... AND TO OUR SOUNDTRACK STUDIO!

Do you love movie and video game music? Do you want to break free from "normal" lessons and try new sounds, new ideas, and even new scales? Do you want to learn to improvise but aren't confident in how to do it?

Welcome to my Mode Crash Course. Modes are a type of scale that many musicians don't understand or are intimidated by. In truth, modes are actually super easy to learn and sound great – making them a secret tool that can unlock great new songs, sounds and ideas for you.

In this book, you will break away from the major scale, unlock the mysteries of modes (and your own imagination) and learn easy-but-powerful melodic patterns that sound amazing. You will be able to use these "Mode Code" patterns to build your melody-making skills and improvise. You are in control of the melodies you create and ways you explore. Let's get started!

SOUNDTRACKS

Imagine you are a soundtrack composer! In each chapter, you'll explore different scenes – film scenes, video game scenes and more – within that mode. You'll even compose and improvise your own songs to the scenes. Together, the songs will form a soundtrack for each mode and get you closer to the grand finale festival: Create-O-Con!

© MERIDEE WINTERS, 2022. ALL RIGHTS RESERVED.   MADE WITH CARE BY REAL HUMANS ✶ CREATE, DON'T COPY

MODE CRASH COURSE

CHAPTER 1 — IONIAN MODE: BASE CAMP

- 2 — Welcome to the Imagination Studio
- 4 — Chord Compass
- 4 — Interval Compass
- 5 — First Pattern Improv
- 6 — Major Adventure
- 7 — Chords of Power

CHAPTER 2 — DORIAN MODE: LEGENDS & QUESTS

- 8 — Dorian Theory
- 10 — Dragon Scales
- 11 — Gregorian Dorian
- 11 — Dragon Improv
- 12 — Legends and Quests
- 13 — Adventure Improv
- 14 — Water and Sky
- 15 — Journey Jam
- 16 — Warrior Heart
- 17 — Warrior Improv

CHAPTER 3 — PHRYGIAN MODE: UNFAMILIAR LANDS

- 20 — Phrygian Theory
- 22 — Descent
- 23 — Roaming Improv
- 23 — Building Suspense
- 24 — Terraform
- 26 — Infinite Mysteries
- 27 — Infinite Improv
- 28 — Ominous Ostinato
- 29 — Ominous Improv

CHAPTER 4 — LYDIAN MODE: DAZZLING DREAMSCAPES

- 32 — Lydian Theory
- 34 — Dream Lands
- 35 — Dream Chords
- 36 — Fantasy Realms
- 37 — Fantasy Realm Improv
- 38 — Flight of Imagination
- 39 — Fluttering Improv
- 40 — Waltz of Wonder
- 40 — Wonder Jam
- 41 — Waltz of Whimsy
- 41 — Whimsical Improv

HOW TO USE THIS BOOK

Theory: Each chapter will begin by teaching you the theory of the mode, the notes in its scale, famous examples of songs in that mode and even tips on how to make that mode sound great.

Patterns and shapes: You will learn by pattern and shape – no need to read music! These songs are built using simple powerful patterns, like:
- Melodic sequences   • Motifs   • Ostinato patterns   • And more!

Create and Explore: There will be prompts to explore and create with these patterns. At any point, you can also break free of the patterns to make your own ideas and improvs.

© MERIDEE WINTERS, 2022. ALL RIGHTS RESERVED.   MADE WITH CARE BY REAL HUMANS ★ CREATE, DON'T COPY

CHAPTER 5 — MIXOLYDIAN MODE: MERRY ADVENTURES

- 44 Mixolydian Theory
- 46 Jig Scale
- 47 Merry Band
- 47 Merry Lands
- 48 Kaleidoscope Skies
- 49 Kaleidoscope Variation
- 50 Fa La La
- 51 Mixolydian Improv
- 52 Jig Jamboree
- 53 Jig Jam Improv

CHAPTER 6 — AEOLIAN MODE: MELANCHOLY & MYSTERY

- 56 Aeolian Theory
- 58 The Sorcerer's Scales
- 60 Mysteries of the Deep
- 60 Deep Dive Improv
- 61 Mystery Waltz
- 61 Mystery Jam
- 62 Moonlight Ostinato
- 63 Moonlight Ostinato: Your Variation
- 64 Night Flight
- 65 Night Flight Improv
- 66 Elf Legend
- 67 Compose Your Own Song

CHAPTER 7 — LOCRIAN MODE: VEXING AND PERPLEXING

- 70 Locrian Theory
- 72 Perplexing Planet
- 73 Interplanetary Improv

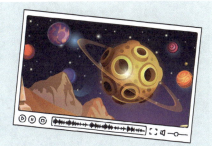

CHAPTER 8 — GRAND FINALE: CREATE-O-CON

- 75 Welcome to Create-o-con
- 76 Event 1: Mode-o-rama
- 78 Event 2: Song-a-thon
- 80 Event 3: Producer-palooza
- 81 Take it Further

Find printable resources at mwfunstuff.com/mode

MODE CRASH COURSE TOOLS

The imagination studio is where you will learn about each mode, get a feel for the sounds and start imagining your own soundtracks and stories.

Image Inspiration: Each mode has images to help inspire your imaginary soundtrack. When you play the piece, imagine the story and characters to help spark your improvisation and creativity.

Helpful Hints: We will coach you on how to play the patterns.

Improv Zones: Using the pattern as a prompt, you will get into the flow and have a chance to improvise your own music.

Improv Timer: The improv timer is your best friend. Meridee's top improv secret is that the best improvisations get into the flow about 2 minutes in. Most people stop improvising too early.

© MERIDEE WINTERS, 2022. ALL RIGHTS RESERVED.   MADE WITH CARE BY REAL HUMANS ★ CREATE, DON'T COPY

Meridee Winters™ Mode Crash Course
© 2006, 2022 BY MERIDEE WINTERS
ISBN: 978-1-943821-77-8

Meridee Winters: Author, Composer, Art Direction
Kate Capps: Editor, Graphic Design, Music Notation
Madé Dimas Wirawan: Comics and Icon Illustrations
Armand Alidio: Cover Design, Additional Design
Special thanks to Krysta Bernhardt for her help in prototyping the first draft and to Kaitlin Borden for sound boarding.

WELCOME TO BASE CAMP!

IONIAN MODE

We'll begin our studies with a mode that will feel familiar. That's because Ionian mode is the same thing as the traditional major scale – the most widely used scale in western music. Soon, we'll break away from the major scale and explore more magical modes. But first, we are going to do a quick review of Ionian and review some basic patterns and concepts that we'll see throughout this book.

Our familiarity with Ionian mode makes it a good starting point, or "base camp" for our mode studies. You can think of this first set of scales and patterns like a map or compass to use as a reference point for the other modes.

Welcome to Ionian mode! Its familiar sound makes it a great starting point!

Ionian mode (a.k.a. the major scale) creates feelings of joy, happiness, playfulness and triumph. It's used in all types of music: classical, popular, theater, children's songs, movie/video soundtracks and more. For this chapter, it's the perfect soundtrack for a triumphant mountain climbing scene. What scenes can you imagine using Ionian for?

P.S. - Don't forget to check out mwfunstuff.com/mode for downloadable versions of the activities in this book!

WELCOME TO THE IMAGINATION STUDIO!

In this studio we'll learn about each mode, list examples of famous songs, practice the scales and even get some tips on how to make the songs and patterns sound great. And before we dig in, let's define what a musical mode actually is!

Mode: a scale (stepwise series of notes) with specific melodic and harmonic properties that give it a distinct sound. The patterns of intervals between each note are always different depending on what mode you are in. Today, only two of the original modes are still commonly used and have been renamed the "major scale" and the "minor scale." They were derived from the Ancient Greek Ionian and Aeolian modes.

1. THE SCALE
Here's the Ionian scale in the key of C. It's just your regular C major scale!

On the keyboard:

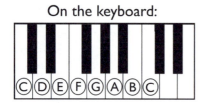

And on the staff:

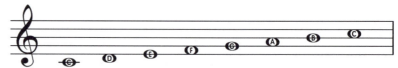

WHOLE WHOLE HALF WHOLE WHOLE WHOLE HALF
(Steps between scale degrees)

2. THE CHORD SCALE
Here's the C Ionian scale as a chord scale.

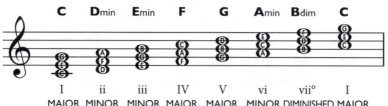

I   ii   iii   IV   V   vi   vii°   I
MAJOR MINOR MINOR MAJOR MAJOR MINOR DIMINISHED MAJOR

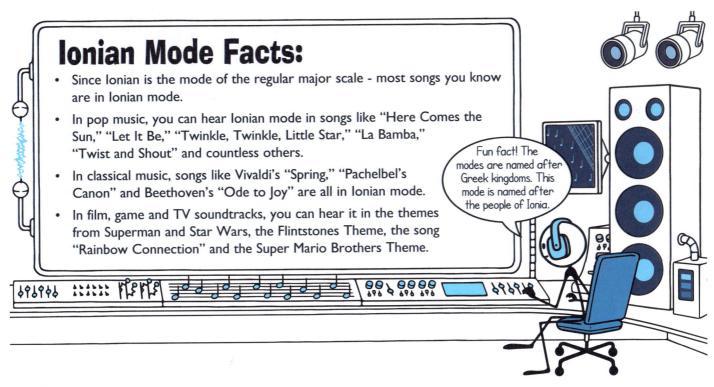

4. HEAR IT: OUR "BASE CAMP" MODE

Ionian mode is the standard major scale we're used to hearing in modern music. Because of that, it's like our "base camp," compass or map – a point of reference to compare against the other modes. Soon, we'll adventure away from the traditional major scale, but first let's review a famous tune. (We'll revisit this song in the book to hear how different it sounds in the different modes.) Here is "On Top of Old Smokey" in Ionian (its normal key/mode).

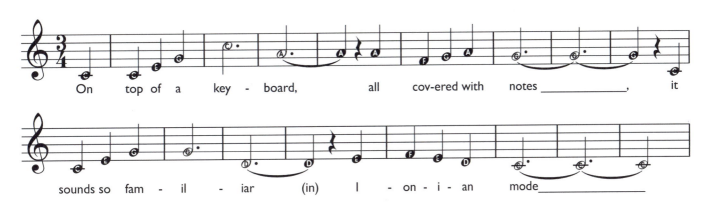

POWER PATTERNS: Here are the patterns from the songs in this chapter. You'll see them throughout the book.

Third: Also called a "skip." A type of interval consisting of two notes with one and a half or two steps in between them. They can be played together or one at a time.

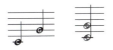

Fifth: A type of interval consisting of two notes with three and a half steps in between them. They can be played together or one at a time.

Arpeggio: A sequence of notes played one after another. In this book our arpeggios are a third and then another third.

Chord: A combination of notes played at the same time. In this book our chords are all triads. (A third with another third, stacked.)

© MERIDEE WINTERS, 2022. ALL RIGHTS RESERVED.   MADE WITH CARE BY REAL HUMANS ★ CREATE, DON'T COPY

#1. CHORD COMPASS

Since Ionian mode is the normal major scale that we're used to hearing, we're going to use it like a compass – a starting point to compare against the other modes. Let's review that major Ionian sound as a soundtrack for this scene – the start of a heroic mountain trek.

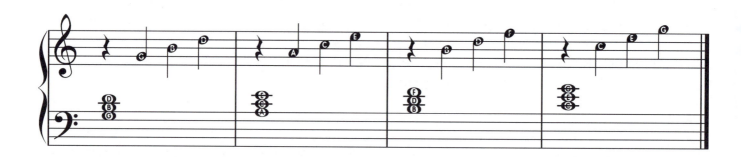

#2. INTERVAL COMPASS

Thirds and fifths are essential patterns used in all songs. They can be parts of chords and parts of melodies. For this song, our left hand will play melodic fifths as an ostinato pattern (a repeating pattern that stays in the same place) while harmonic thirds climb up the scale.

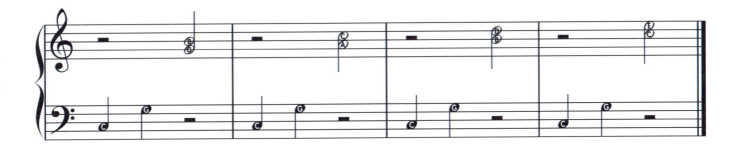

#3. FIRST PATTERN IMPROV

Now we will play an improv using a "pattern prompt." In creative writing, authors often start with a writing prompt and do a timed exercise. Our improvs will have a prompt and instructions to play for 3 minutes.

Now, keep playing the root-fifth pattern with your left hand while your right hand improvises however you want. Finger paint the keys - there are no wrong notes!

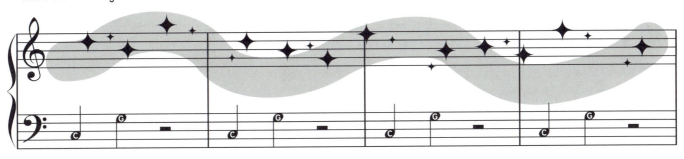

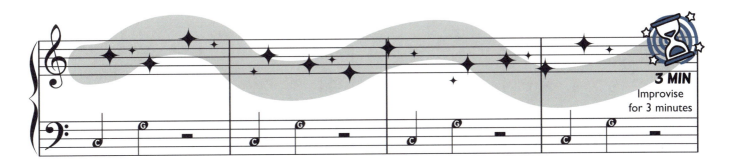

3 MIN
Improvise for 3 minutes

#4. MAJOR ADVENTURE

This Ionian chord progression uses the "one," "four" and "five" chords from the chord scale. These chords are used in combination in thousands of pop and folk songs and get their own chapter in our Chord Quest 3 Book!

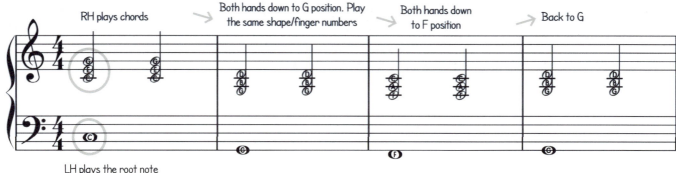

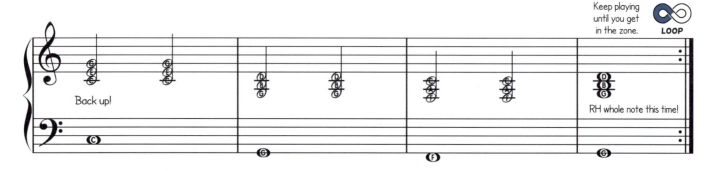

#5. CHORDS OF POWER

This Ionian chord progression is like a pop music "secret weapon" also used in tons of hit pop and rock songs, from "Don't Stop Believin'" to "Can You Feel the Love Tonight" and countless others. It gets its own Chapter in Chord Quest 2!

Make it a duet! Have someone make up a melody on the white keys while you play this progression.

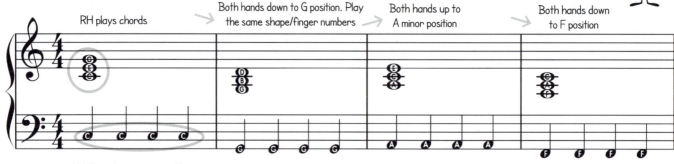

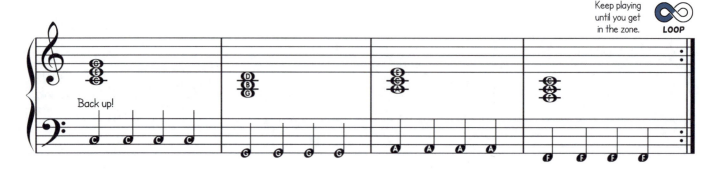

CHAPTER 2

DORIAN MODE

LET'S GET LEGENDARY IN DORIAN MODE!

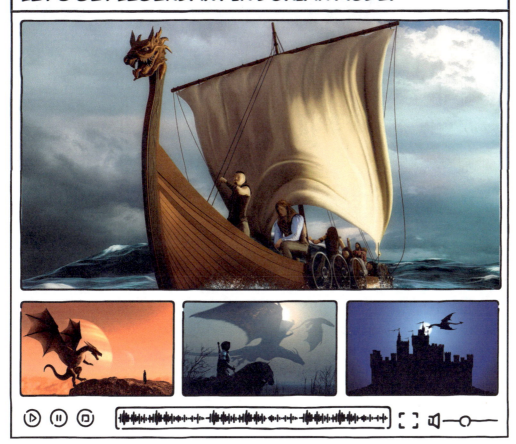

Moving just one key away from Ionian mode creates a big change in possibilities. We are now entering the mythic mood of Dorian mode. The half step between the second and third notes and the whole step between the seventh and eighth notes make this scale sound minor yet powerful, sometimes melancholy... but always legendary.

Dorian Mode is widely used in soundtracks with images of castles, battles, medieval times, quests, legends and more. What movies or video games have you seen with these themes?

Welcome to Dorian Mode! A perfect mode for heroic adventures.

Important: You are on your own adventure. Be a brave explorer. The scenes, images and improvisation prompts in this book are here to spark your own imagination. What music and images can you imagine? Write or record your ideas. Then share your imaginary (or real) soundtracks with others.

DORIAN MODE: Theory

Dorian mode: the scale of medieval-sounding legends, quests and... dragons.

1. THE SCALE
Here's the Dorian scale in the key of D.

On the keyboard: D E F G A B C D

And on the staff: D E F G A B C D

2. THE CHORD SCALE
Here's the D Dorian scale as a chord scale.

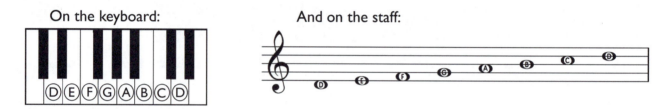

Dmin	Emin	F	G	Amin	Bdim	C	Dmin
i	ii	III	IV	v	vi°	VII	i
MINOR	MINOR	MAJOR	MAJOR	MINOR	DIMINISHED	MAJOR	MINOR

3. NOTABLE INTERVALS
Here are the intervals of the scale that give Dorian Mode its unique sound:

Lowered seventh   Minor third   Major sixth

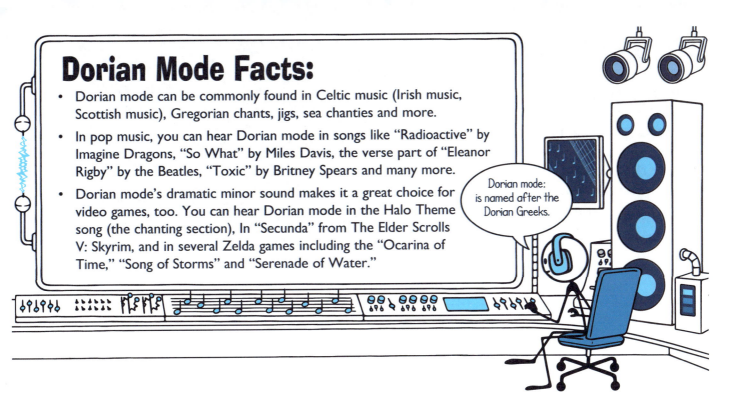

4. HEAR THE DIFFERENCE

Here is "On Top of Old Smokey" in Dorian mode.

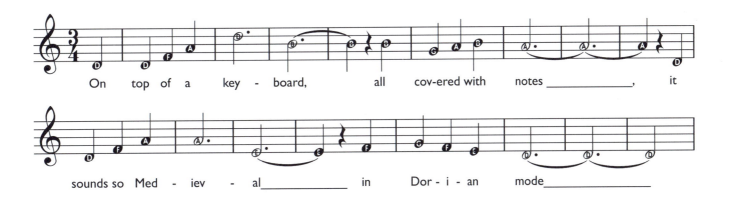

Try these sounds and effects with Dorian mode. Some are cinematic and dramatic, and some were used in the Middle Ages.

- On a piano, try adding pedal for a flowing effect.
- If using a keyboard, try flutes, pan flute, bagpipes, recorder, fiddle and violin for authentic medieval sounds.
- Try trumpet and horn sounds with "Gregorian Dorian" for a castle feel.
- Voice and choir pads sound ancient, mysterious and dramatic. (Try several, as some don't sound great.)
- Try accordion for a pirate sound!
- Avoid: modern, synth or high-tech sounds, electric organs or keyboard sounds.

#6. DRAGON SCALES

Every great scene and every great soundtrack tells a story. What story can you imagine here? Move up the Dorian scale with a simple melodic sequence in your right hand, while your left hand goes up the scale playing harmonic fifths. Then climb back down the scale!

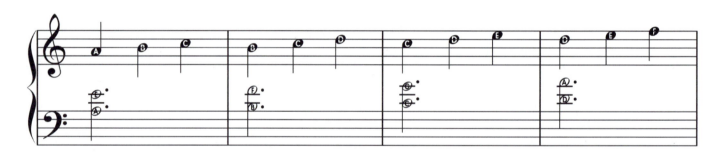

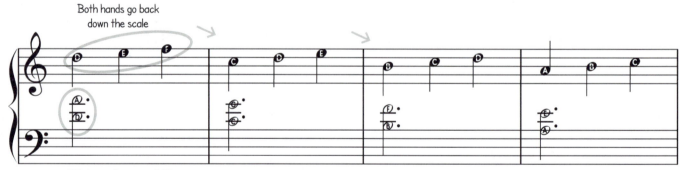

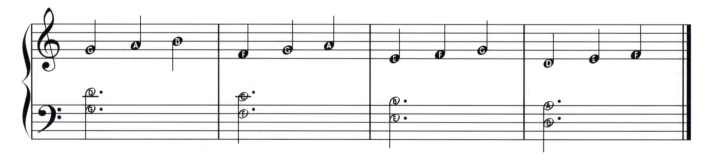

#7. GREGORIAN DORIAN

Your hands will play parallel harmonic fifths in this medieval-sounding tune!

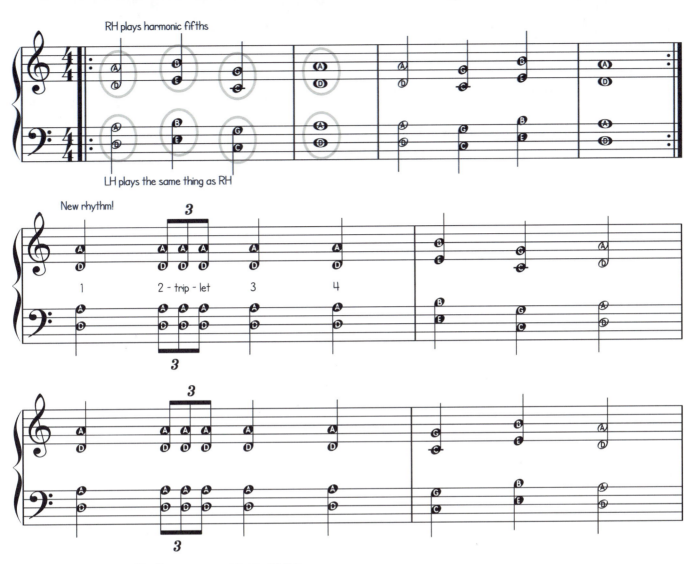

#8. DRAGON IMPROV

Now improvise all over using parallel fifths....

Improvise for 3 minutes

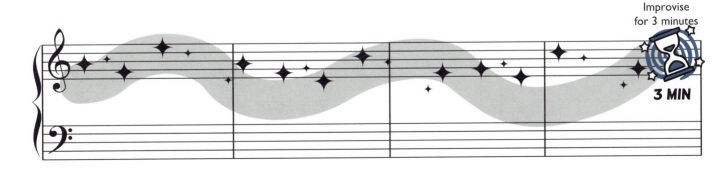

#9. LEGENDS AND QUESTS

In this song, a 3/4 time melodic sequence supported by droning left hand chords drives a sense of motion forward. This combination is perfect for galloping horses, flying dragons, sea chanties, jigs or viking ships! What adventure do you imagine?

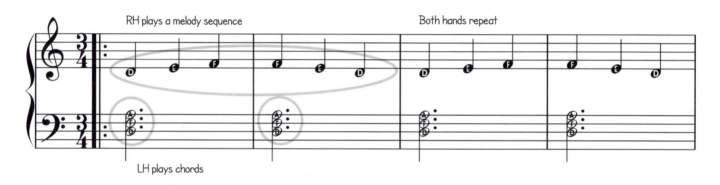

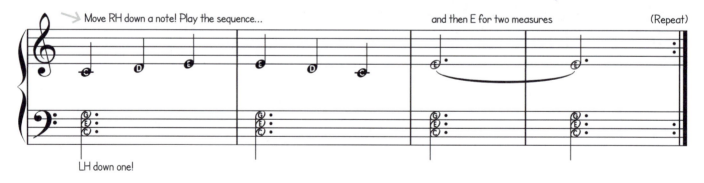

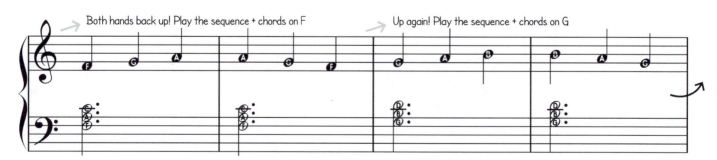

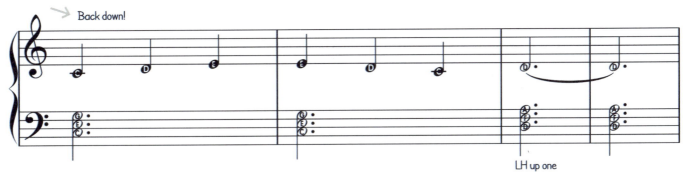

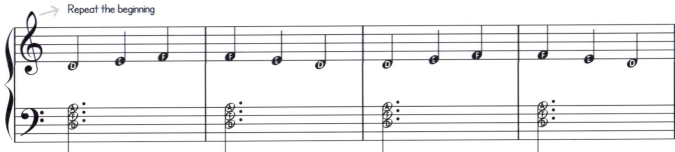

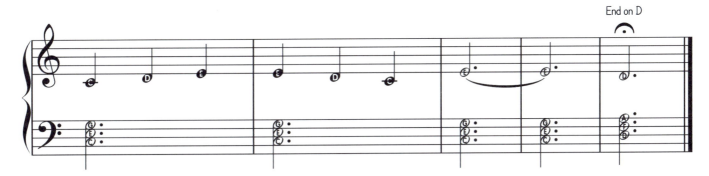

#10. ADVENTURE IMPROV

Create your own adventure! Jam for 3 minutes and narrate your own story. Where will your imagination take you? Your left hand can play chords that move around, repeated D minor chords, or whatever you choose!

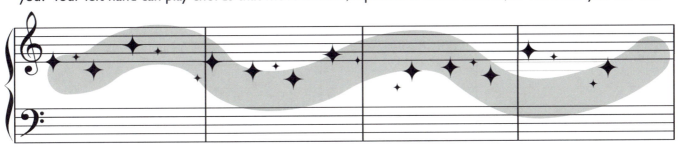

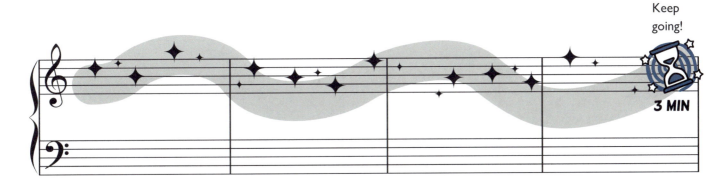

#11. WATER AND SKY

Get into the flow as you imagine a journey across sea and sky. Your right hand will play a simple melody while your left hand moves between D minor and C arpeggios.

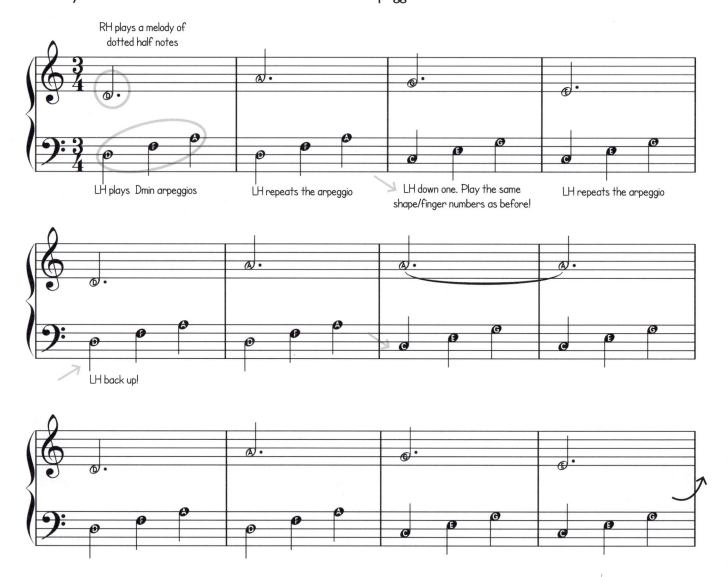

#12. JOURNEY JAM

Take your imagination for a ride as you dream up your own adventure scenes and jam to visions of the sea or sky. Improvise your own right hand melody as your left hand plays repeating D minor arpeggios. Keep going for 3 minutes (no matter what). Hint: if you feel stuck, ask yourself "what happens next?" and play that as you narrate.

#13. WARRIOR HEART

This mythical-sounding song has been a favorite at Meridee's music school for decades. Your left hand plays a melodic fifth, and your right hand echoes with a melodic third. Together, they tell a story of adventure and triumph.

#14. WARRIOR IMPROV

Now improvise using that same shape/sequence of a melodic fifth then melodic third. What story does your song tell?

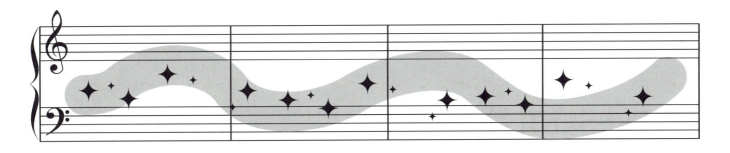

Keep going!

3 MIN

YOU ARE THE PRODUCER!

Music producers are great at prototyping — meaning they make an initial version of something and continue to evolve it into something great. Before moving onto the next mode, prototype an idea inspired by your Dorian mode adventures. Then share it with others!

Great music producers try out ideas, get feedback and evolve their project!

#1) CAPTURE

Pick one idea. Now get the rough idea down in some form - a recording, writing notes about it, notating the music or however works for you! Choose a method to capture your idea below.

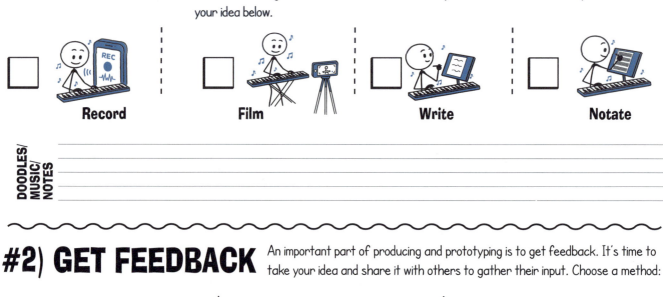

☐ Record   ☐ Film   ☐ Write   ☐ Notate

DOODLES/ MUSIC/ NOTES
_____
_____
_____
_____

#2) GET FEEDBACK

An important part of producing and prototyping is to get feedback. It's time to take your idea and share it with others to gather their input. Choose a method:

☐  Play a recording   ☐  Play a video   ☐  Perform for Others

FEEDBACK/ NOTES

#3) PRESENT!

Take the feedback you received and use it to improve your idea! Once you've got a version you like, share it with others. Choose one of the methods below to share your piece, whether that's making a more polished video or putting on a show! (P.S. - even if it's a short song, a small idea or an imperfect in-process song, sharing is still rewarding and might even inspire others.)

☐  Simple Recording   ☐  Homemade Movie   ☐  Soundtrack   ☐  Written song   ☐  Show

Congratulations! You're ready to move on to Chapter 3!

Psst! Find a printable download of this page at mwfunstuff.com/mode

CHAPTER 3
PHRYGIAN MODE

LET'S EXPLORE AND CREATE SOME MYSTERIES...

As we step up the keys, we arrive at the mysterious and powerful sounds of Phrygian Mode.

Phrygian mode has a minor sound, but the half step between the first and second notes of the scale also conjure images of unexplored landscapes, ancient deserts, stars, mountains, canyons... and maybe even a mysterious creature or two.

This mode is perfect for your next soundtrack project: a score to convey the suspenseful feelings of exploring an intriguing, unknown world.

Welcome to Phrygian Mode! This mode is perfect for exploring a mysterious landscape!

PHRYGIAN MODE: Theory

Phrygian mode is minor and ominous. Perfect for songs about unexplored places.

1. THE SCALE
Here's the Phrygian scale in the key of E.

On the keyboard:

And on the staff:

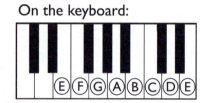

HALF   WHOLE WHOLE WHOLE HALF   WHOLE WHOLE
(Steps between scale degrees)

2. THE CHORD SCALE
Here's the E Phrygian scale as a chord scale.

Emin	F	G	Amin	Bdim	C	Dmin	Emin
i	II	III	iv	v°	VI	vii	i
MINOR	MAJOR	MAJOR	MINOR	DIMINISHED	MAJOR	MINOR	MINOR

3. NOTABLE INTERVALS
Here are the parts of the scale that give Phrygian mode its unique sound.

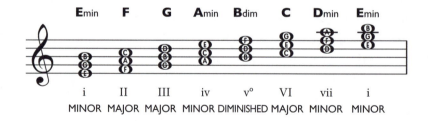

Half step between the first and second scale degrees

Minor third

Lowered/minor seventh

Phrygian Mode Facts:

- Phrygian mode sounds powerful and mysterious because of the strong-sounding half step between the first and second degree of the scale. It also has a flat 7th and a minor third. It is a minor mode.
- Phrygian mode is used in many cultures - Spanish, Neoclassical, the Maqam melodic system of Arabic, Persian and Turkish classical music, the Bhairavi scale in Indian classical music, Western "Hard Rock" music and more.
- Some famous songs that use Phrygian mode are "Would" by Alice in Chains, "London Calling" by the Clash, "Bachannale" from the opera "Samson and Delilah" and the prelude from the Lord of the Rings Soundtrack.

Phrygian mode is named after the ancient Anatolian kingdom, Phrygia.

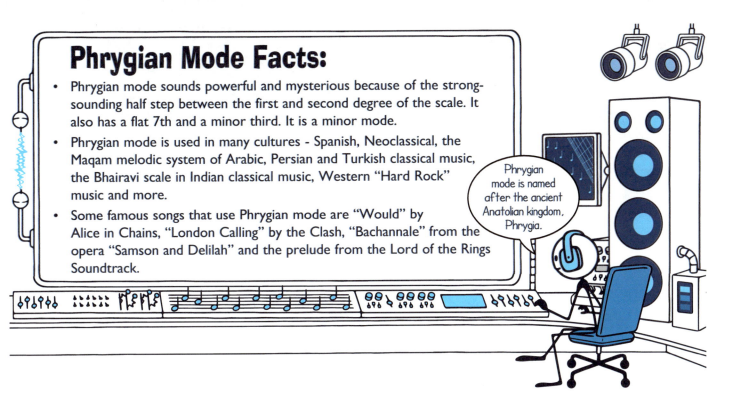

4. HEAR THE DIFFERENCE

Here is "On Top of Old Smokey" in Phrygian Mode. How does it sound different than the normal version?

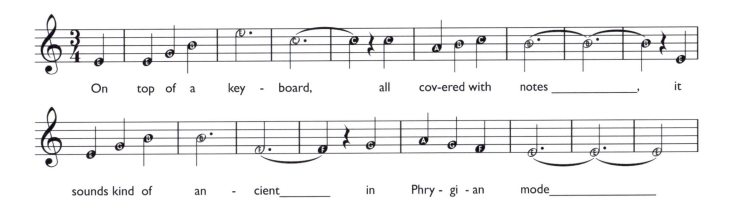

On top of a key-board, all cov-ered with notes _____, it sounds kind of an-cient _____ in Phry-gi-an mode _____

Here are some effects, keyboard sounds and instruments to use with Phrygian mode.

- **Phrygian mode** is well suited for keyboard sounds that are cinematic, ancient or global (or even interplanetary!).
- **Try keyboard sounds** like orchestral strings for a lush sound, choral voices for a mysterious or ancient sound, synth pads for an otherworldly sound or electric guitar for a heavy metal sound.
- **Phrygian mode is used in many cultures,** so sounds from those regions work great as well. Try oboe, flutes and more.
- **Add accompaniment** like timpani, dumbek or udu.
- **Avoid traditional or bright sounds** like calliope or electric piano.
- **Try playing Phrygian songs and improvs with a raised third.** This is called the Altered Phrygian or Freygish scale and is used in Indian, Middle Eastern, Eastern European, Central Asian, flamenco music and more.

#15. DESCENT

This scalar piece descends the Phrygian scale using patterns of seconds. Seconds are neighbor notes that can build tension. This is because seconds want to move, wander and resolve.

#16. ROAMING IMPROV

Be adventurous and let your fingers and imagination roam. What mysterious images come to your mind? For this improv, your left hand continues the repeating fifths pattern from the last song. Your right hand can roam around as it improvises a melody. Remember: improvise for 3 minutes or more!

Keep going! 3 MIN

#17. BUILDING SUSPENSE

Seconds can be used to build suspense. (Check out the theme from Jaws for a great example!) This song plays melodic fifths, but moves up and down a step (a.k.a. a second) from measure to measure. To add to the suspense, start quietly and slowly, growing faster and louder as you play.

LH plays a fifth. Then RH. Up one! Just play the same shape/finger numbers. Down one!

Keep repeating, growing faster and louder!

© MERIDEE WINTERS, 2022. ALL RIGHTS RESERVED. MADE WITH CARE BY REAL HUMANS ★ CREATE, DON'T COPY

#18. TERRAFORM

Fifths are such solid building blocks that they are called "perfect fifths." They can be found often in rock music. This song uses a variety of fifths in different patterns.

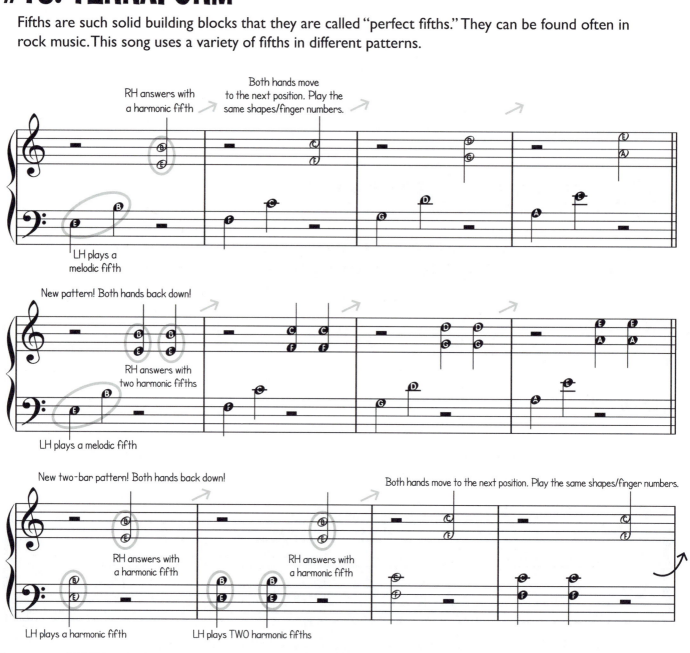

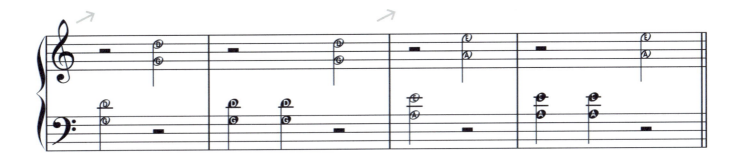

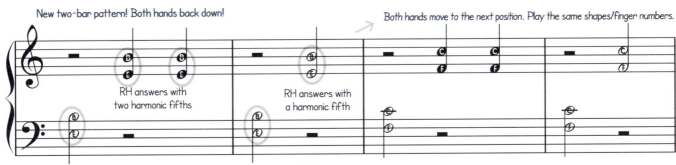

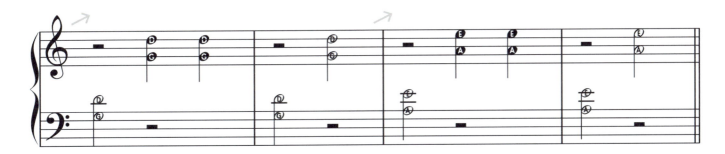

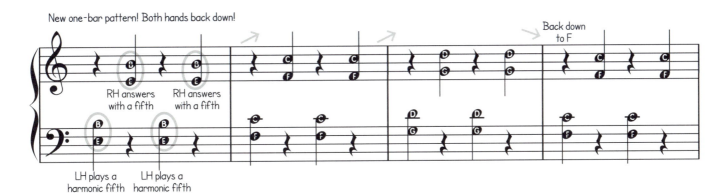

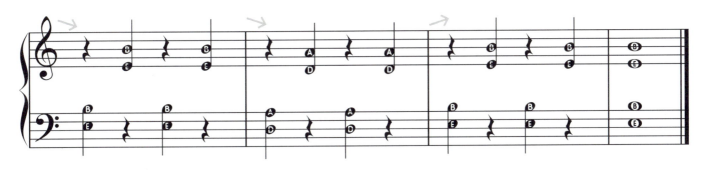

#19. INFINITE MYSTERIES

This intriguing tune features right hand whole note fifths played over a repeating left hand fifth pattern. Your left hand stays in place while your right hand moves around!

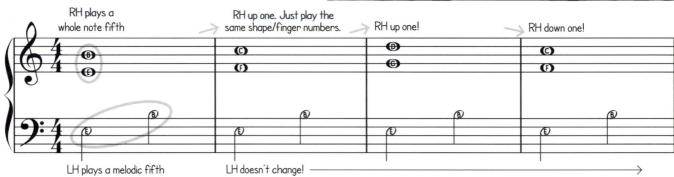

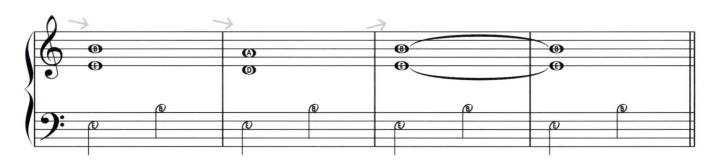

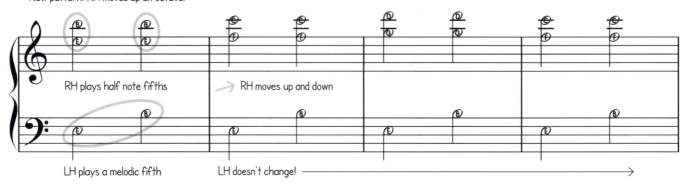

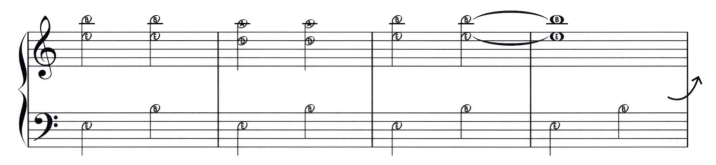

Back to RH whole notes. Now the RH moves down the scale

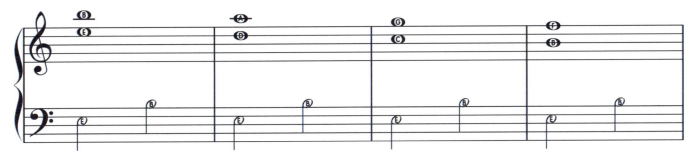

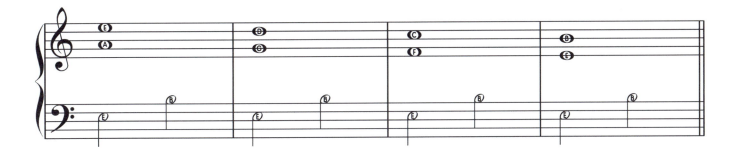

#20. INFINITE IMPROV

Music and imagination are both infinite. When you improvise, you can create and imagine new worlds. For this improv, your left hand can continue the repeating half-note fifths pattern from the last song. Your right hand can improvise a mystical melody. What are you imagining?

Keep going!

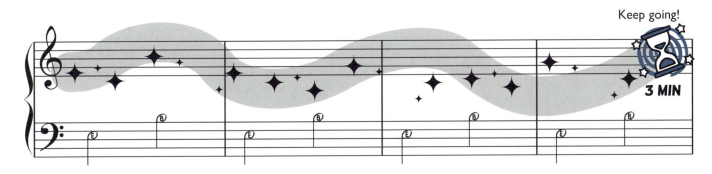

3 MIN

#21. OMINOUS OSTINATO

Something is emerging from the shadows with this song. Your left hand will play an ominous ostinato part (repeating the same notes in the same place) while your right hand plays a whole note melody.

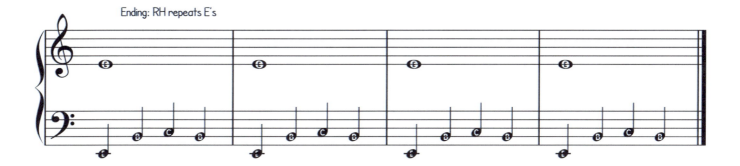

#22. OMINOUS IMPROV

Your left hand will play the same ostinato pattern from the last song. Your right hand can explore all over and improvise a mysterious melody.

YOU ARE THE PRODUCER!

Music producers are great at prototyping – meaning they make an initial version of something and continue to evolve it into something great. Before moving onto the next mode, prototype an idea inspired by your Phrygian mode adventures. Then share it with others!

Great music producers try out ideas, get feedback and evolve their project!

#1) CAPTURE

Pick one idea. Now get the rough idea down in some form - a recording, writing notes about it, notating the music or however works for you! Choose a method to capture your idea below.

☐ Record   ☐ Film   ☐ Write   ☐ Notate

DOODLES/MUSIC/NOTES
_____
_____
_____
_____

#2) GET FEEDBACK

An important part of producing and prototyping is to get feedback. It's time to take your idea and share it with others to gather their input. Choose a method:

☐ Play a recording   ☐ Play a video   ☐ Perform for Others

FEEDBACK/NOTES

#3) PRESENT!

Take the feedback you received and use it to improve your idea! Once you've got a version you like, share it with others. Choose one of the methods below to share your piece, whether that's making a more polished video or putting on a show! (P.S. - even if it's a short song, a small idea or an imperfect in-process song, sharing is still rewarding and might even inspire others.)

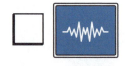    

☐ Simple Recording   ☐ Homemade Movie   ☐ Soundtrack   ☐ Written song   ☐ Show

Congratulations! You're ready to move on to Chapter 4!

Psst! Find a printable download of this page at mwfunstuff.com/mode

LYDIAN MODE

CHAPTER 4

NOW FOR DREAMY, ETHEREAL LYDIAN MODE!

Welcome to Lydian mode, which conjures images of imagined lands, quirky characters, surreal dreams and even the occasional dark fairy tale. Lydian is a major mode, but with more dreaminess and quirk than the straightforward major-scale happiness of Ionian. While Phrygian was minor, strong and mysterious. Lydian is major and a bit strange (thanks to its raised fourth scale degree) – but in a good and almost blissful way.

Lydian mode is used by composers to capture feelings like wonder, awe, magic and playfulness. When thinking of Lydian, imagine characters that are unusual yet charming. Imagine dark fairy tales, dream scenes and even surreal miracles. Or imagine the weird playfulness of the Simpson's Theme (which was written in a variation of Lydian mode).

Welcome to Lydian Mode! This dreamy mode is perfect for otherworldly landscapes!

Your mission for this chapter is to improvise dreamscapes to enchanting scenes and even imagine your own worlds and characters. How far can you stretch your imagination? What other scenes do you imagine exist in Lydian mode?

1. THE SCALE
Here's the Lydian scale in the key of F.

On the keyboard: F G A B C D E F

And on the staff: F G A B C D E F

WHOLE WHOLE WHOLE HALF WHOLE WHOLE HALF
(Steps between scale degrees)

2. THE CHORD SCALE
Here's the F Lydian scale as a chord scale.

F — G — Amin — Bdim — C — Dmin — Emin — F
I — II — iii — iv° — V — vi — vii — i
MAJOR MAJOR MINOR DIMINISHED MAJOR MINOR MINOR MINOR

3. NOTABLE INTERVALS
Lydian mode has just one note different than the typical major scale (Ionian mode): a raised fourth.

Augmented (raised) fourth

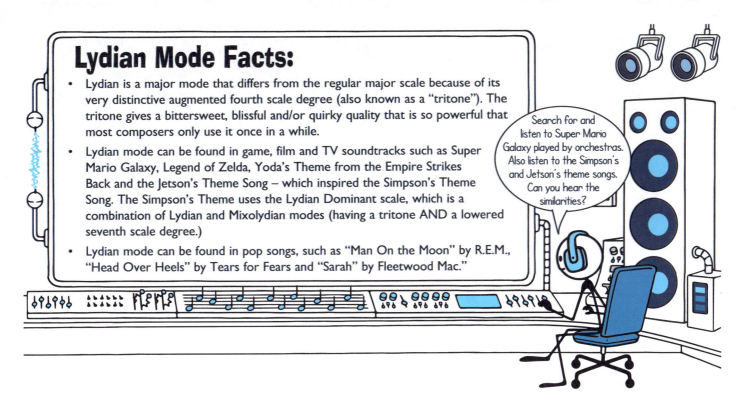

Lydian Mode Facts:

- Lydian is a major mode that differs from the regular major scale because of its very distinctive augmented fourth scale degree (also known as a "tritone"). The tritone gives a bittersweet, blissful and/or quirky quality that is so powerful that most composers only use it once in a while.
- Lydian mode can be found in game, film and TV soundtracks such as Super Mario Galaxy, Legend of Zelda, Yoda's Theme from the Empire Strikes Back and the Jetson's Theme Song – which inspired the Simpson's Theme Song. The Simpson's Theme uses the Lydian Dominant scale, which is a combination of Lydian and Mixolydian modes (having a tritone AND a lowered seventh scale degree.)
- Lydian mode can be found in pop songs, such as "Man On the Moon" by R.E.M., "Head Over Heels" by Tears for Fears and "Sarah" by Fleetwood Mac."

Search for and listen to Super Mario Galaxy played by orchestras. Also listen to the Simpson's and Jetson's theme songs. Can you hear the similarities?

4. HEAR THE DIFFERENCE

Here is "On Top of Old Smokey" in Lydian Mode.

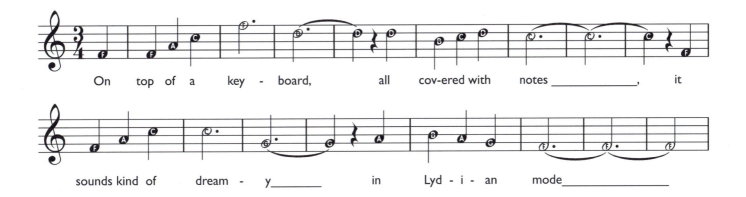

On top of a key-board, all cov-ered with notes_____, it sounds kind of dream-y_____ in Lyd-i-an mode_____

Here are some effects, keyboard sounds and instruments to use with Lydian mode.

- **For Lydian sound effects,** look for sounds/effects that evoke a sense of childlike wonder and awe, quirky characters with unique charms or dark (but not super scary) fairy tales.
- **Add pedal** to accentuate the dreamy, flowing sound of Lydian mode.
- **Use dynamics -** build from quiet to loud, or slowly get quieter as if drifting off to sleep or floating away.
- **Choose keyboard sound thats evoke wonder:** lush or textural sounds with lots of sparkle (and lots of reverb).
- **Try rich synth pad sounds,** like ice chimes, bells, harps or layered sounds, or **New Age type sounds.**
- **Avoid sounds** that are harsh, intense or even "normal" sounding like horns, clarinet, saxophone, organ, electric guitar or electric piano.

#23. DREAM LANDS

Warm up your wonder with arpeggios exploring the Lydian scale. Can you hear and feel the magic? To play, move down the Lydian scale with arpeggios in your right hand, while your left hand stays in one spot playing F major arpeggios.

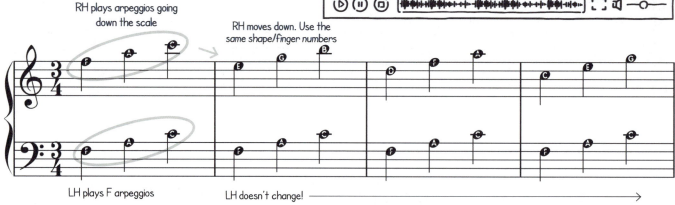

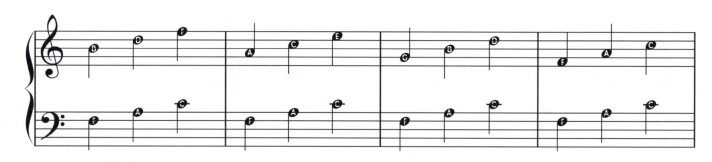

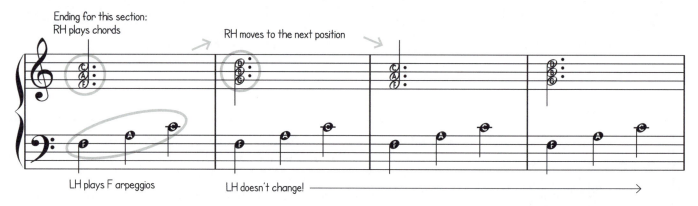

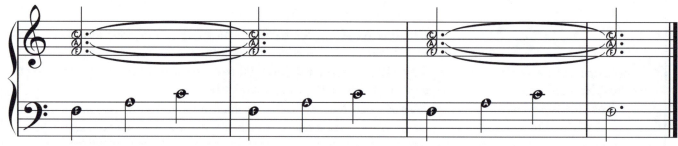

#24. DREAM CHORDS: PEDAL POINT PATTERN 1

This type of pedal point pattern was a favorite trick for bands like Fleetwood Mac. Read more below!

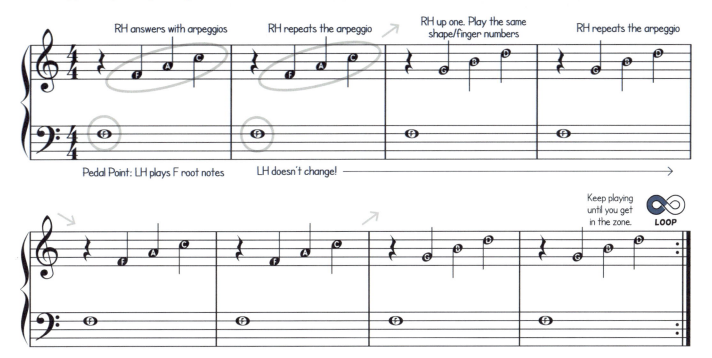

#25. DREAM CHORDS: PEDAL POINT PATTERN 2

This pedal point song features chords in the RH and quarter note root notes in the LH.

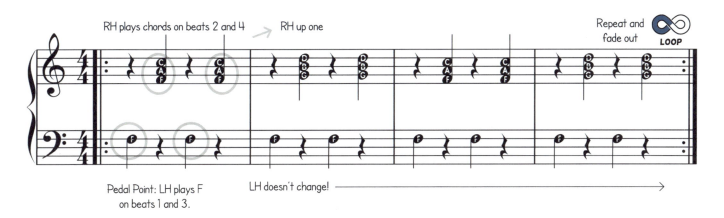

PEDAL POINT

"Pedal point" is the term for a single continued or sustained note (usually the bottom note) in music that has other harmonies change over it.

Both the songs above use a pedal point of F in the bass clef!

Pedal point can be found in classical music, but also in pop, rock and more.

#26. FANTASY REALMS

In this flowing, floating song, your right hand will dreamily explore the keys with harmonic thirds while your left hand stays in one place, playing F major arpeggios.

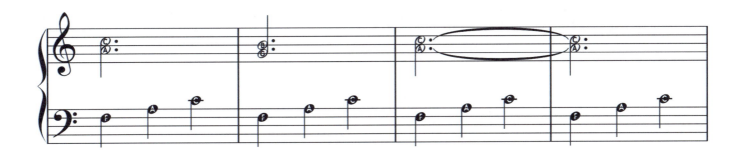

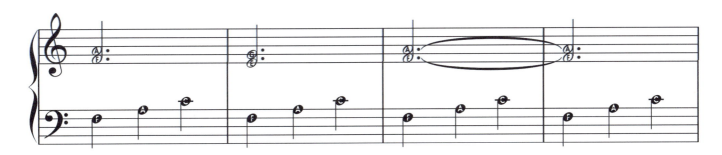

#27. FANTASY REALM IMPROV

This is Meridee's favorite improv prompt because it is not just dreamy but also has a heartfelt harmonious quality. How long can you stay in flow? What do you feel? What do you imagine?

Left hand plays repeating F major arpeggios.

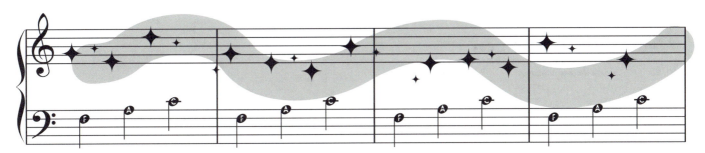

Keep going!

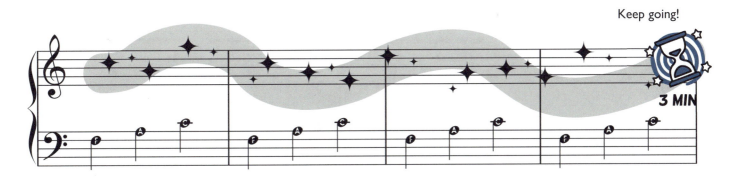

3 MIN

#28. FLIGHT OF IMAGINATION

Flutter around the keys! Your left hand will play F chords while your right hand flutters with thirds.

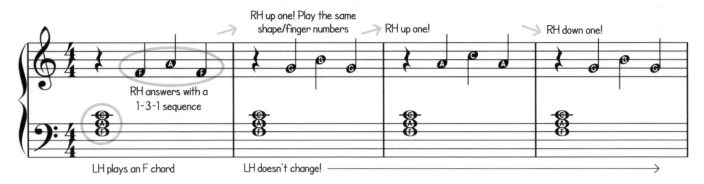
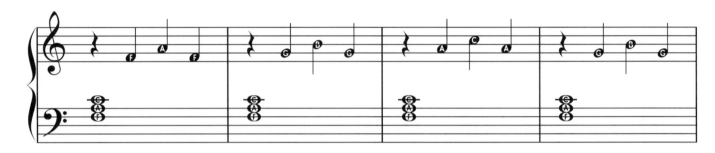
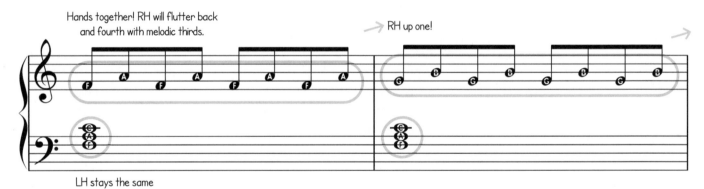
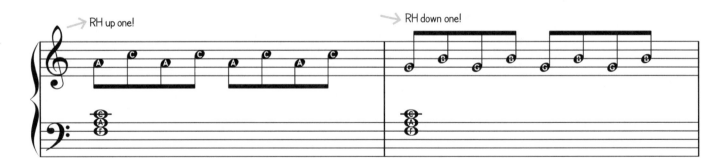
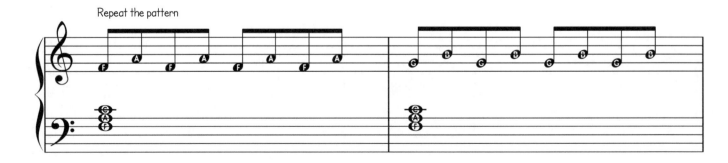

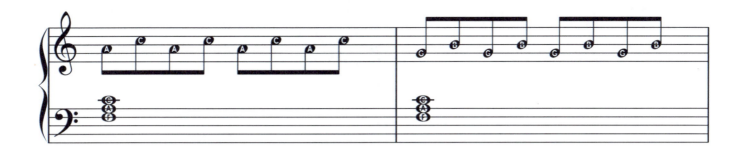

Repeat the first section/pattern

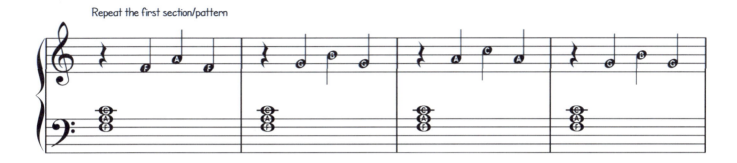

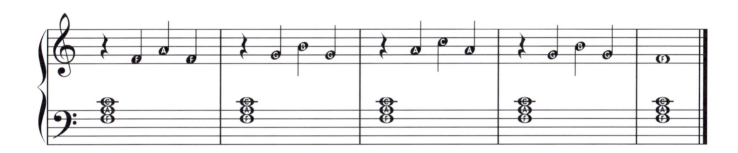

#29. FLUTTERING IMPROV

Now improvise! Flutter around with your right hand while your left hand continues playing F chords.

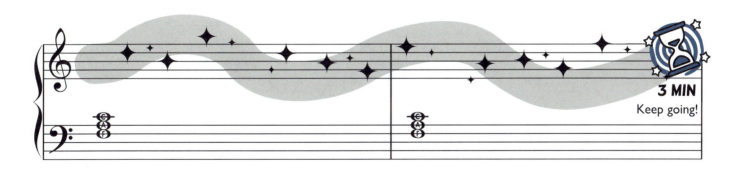

3 MIN
Keep going!

#30. WALTZ OF WONDER

Take to the skies in this lighthearted tune. Your left hand will repeat F major arpeggios while your right hand floats through a simple melody. Then improvise your own melody over the pattern!

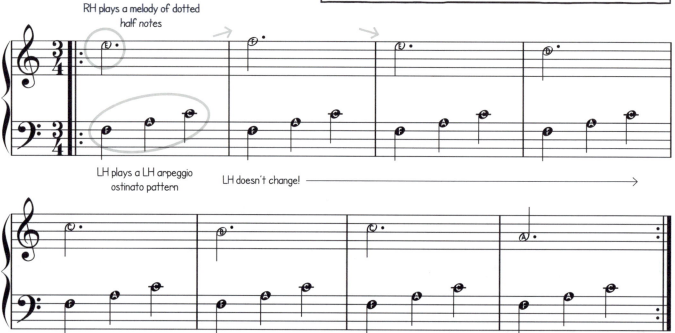

#31. WONDER JAM

Now improvise your own melody that moves around over that same LH arpeggio pattern. Try adding pedal to make it extra flowy.

Keep going!

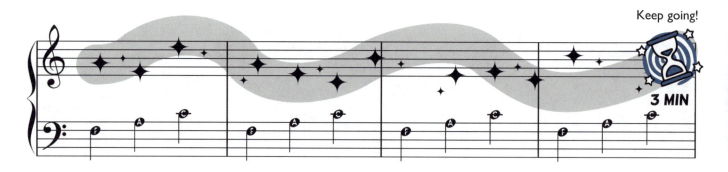

3 MIN

#32. WALTZ OF WHIMSY

Changing just the left hand pattern can change this waltz from a flowing, dreamy song into a playful one. Here, your right hand will play the Waltz of Wonder melody over a LH "Oom-Pah-Pah" Pattern.

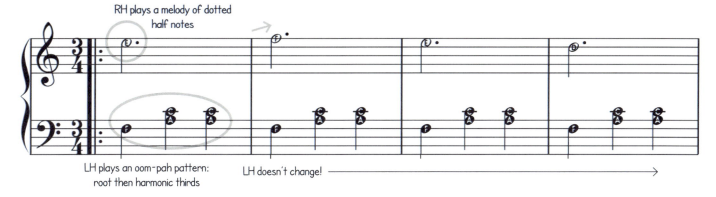

RH plays a melody of dotted half notes

LH plays an oom-pah pattern: root then harmonic thirds

LH doesn't change!

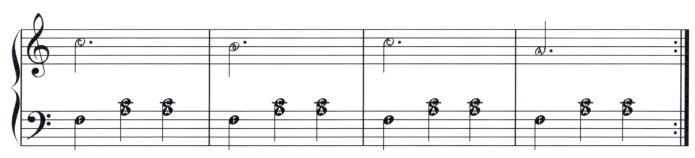

#33. WHIMSICAL IMPROV

Now improvise your own whimsical melody that moves around over the same LH oom-pah-pah pattern.

Learn more about (and play!) Oom-pah music in Chord Quest 2!

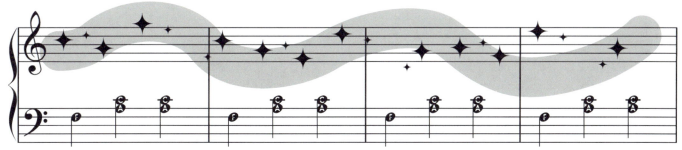

Keep going!

3 MIN

© MERIDEE WINTERS, 2022. ALL RIGHTS RESERVED.   MADE WITH CARE BY REAL HUMANS ★ CREATE, DON'T COPY

YOU ARE THE PRODUCER!

Music producers are great at prototyping — meaning they make an initial version of something and continue to evolve it into something great. Before moving onto the next mode, prototype an idea inspired by your Lydian mode adventures. Then share it with others!

Great music producers try out ideas, get feedback and evolve their project!

#1) CAPTURE

Pick one idea. Now get the rough idea down in some form - a recording, writing notes about it, notating the music or however works for you! Choose a method to capture your idea below.

☐ Record ☐ Film ☐ Write ☐ Notate

DOODLES/ MUSIC/ NOTES
_____
_____
_____
_____

#2) GET FEEDBACK

An important part of producing and prototyping is to get feedback. It's time to take your idea and share it with others to gather their input. Choose a method:

☐ Play a recording ☐ Play a video ☐ Perform for Others

FEEDBACK/ NOTES

#3) PRESENT!

Take the feedback you received and use it to improve your idea! Once you've got a version you like, share it with others. Choose one of the methods below to share your piece, whether that's making a more polished video or putting on a show! (P.S. - even if it's a short song, a small idea or an imperfect in-process song, sharing is still rewarding and might even inspire others.)

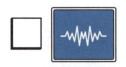    

☐ Simple Recording ☐ Homemade Movie ☐ Soundtrack ☐ Written song ☐ Show

Congratulations! You're ready to move on to Chapter 5!

Psst! Find a printable download of this page at mwfunstuff.com/mode

CHAPTER 5

MIXOLYDIAN

Mixolydian is a happy, major mode – but with a bit more character than the straightforward major-scale happiness of Ionian. Unlike Dorian (which was minor and legendary), or Phrygian (which was minor and mysterious) or Lydian (which was major yet strange) – Mixolydian is major and versatile.

The raised third note of the Mixolydian scale gives it the positive, lighthearted sound common to all the major modes, but the lowered seventh (the only note different than the Ionian scale) gives it flexibility to sound bluesy, rocking or even medieval. It is used in video games and movies atop scenes of festive villages, used in rock music to convey a happy bittersweet feeling, and is even the primary preferred tuning of Celtic bagpipes.

Welcome to Mixolydian Mode — perfect for enchanted worlds and elf-inspired jigs!

The Mixolydian mode is perfect for your next project – the soundtrack for a fun-filled video game of merry villages, bright blue skies and magical landscapes (bagpipes optional).

MIXOLYDIAN MODE: Theory

Mixolydian mode is major and playful - perfect for the merry world of these scenes!

1. THE SCALE
Here's the Mixolydian scale in the key of G.

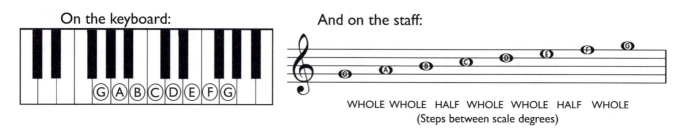

On the keyboard: G A B C D E F G

And on the staff: G A B C D E F G

WHOLE WHOLE HALF WHOLE WHOLE HALF WHOLE
(Steps between scale degrees)

2. THE CHORD SCALE
Here's the G Mixolydian scale as a chord scale.

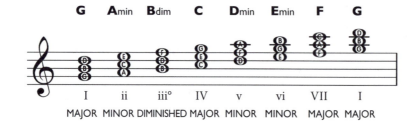

G   Amin   Bdim   C   Dmin   Emin   F   G

I   ii   iii°   IV   v   vi   VII   I

MAJOR   MINOR   DIMINISHED   MAJOR   MINOR   MINOR   MAJOR   MAJOR

3. NOTABLE INTERVALS
Here is the interval that gives Mixolydian its unique sound, played going up and going down:

Lowered seventh/minor seventh   Lowered seventh (going down)

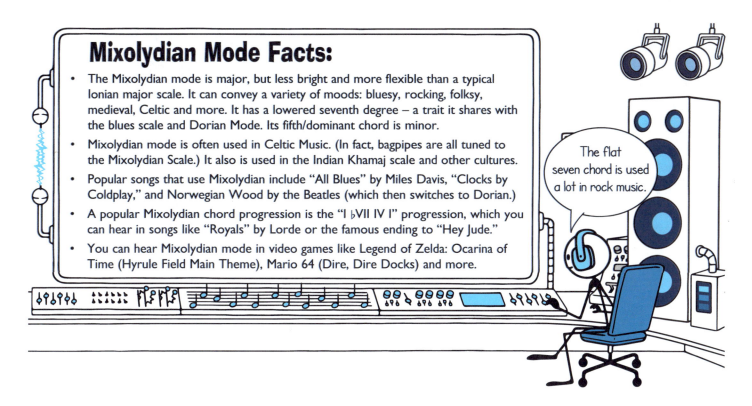

4. HEAR THE DIFFERENCE

Here is the familiar tune of "Happy Birthday" in Mixolydian mode. The only notes that are different are the F's!

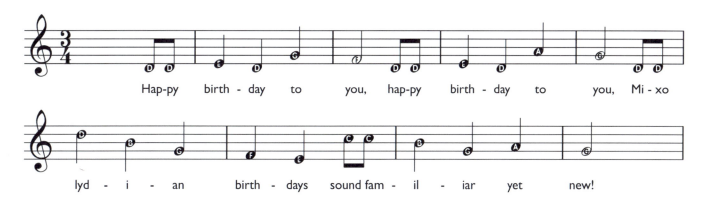

Hap-py birth-day to you, hap-py birth-day to you, Mi-xo-lyd-i-an birth-days sound fam-il-iar yet new!

Here are some tips, effects and keyboard sounds to use with Mixolydian mode.

- **Because Mixolydian can sound medieval and folksy (like a happier, brighter Dorian) or can sound more melancholy than the Ionian major scale, it has a variety of uses.** You can choose similar sounds to Dorian mode or pick cute, fun sounds that work for video games. Have fun with it!
- **Medieval keyboard sounds:** try flutes, bagpipes, pan flute, recorder, fiddle and violin for authentic medieval sounds.
- **Cinematic sounds:** try lush strings or orchestra sounds
- **Video game sounds:** bright synth sounds, slightly cheesy synth sounds, calliope, marimba, toy piano, electric organ and more.

#34. JIG SCALE

Welcome to this enchanted scene! Move up the G mixolydian scale with this festive jig pattern. Your left hand will stay in the same place for the whole song playing a droning harmonic fifth. (Read more about drones below!)

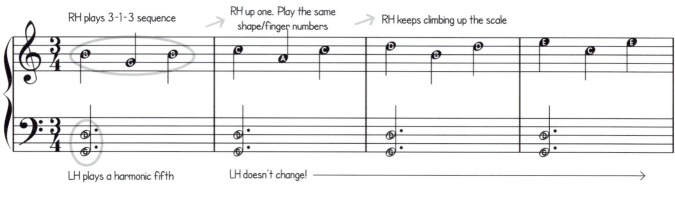

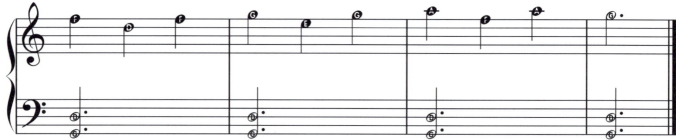

DRONE

A drone is a type of accompaniment where a single chord, note or harmonic interval is continuously played throughout all or most of a piece. It is similar to pedal point (which we learned about in the last chapter), but pedal points can be shorter passages and are usually a single note, whereas a drone can be a note, multiple notes or a chord and typically last for an entire song.

In the song above, the left hand plays a drone of G and D (a harmonic fifth) while the right hand changes notes.

#35. MERRY BAND

This cheerful song focuses on the signature harmonic move in Mixolydian mode: the tonic note (G) down to the "flat 7" (F). Try recording yourself playing it and then improvising to the recording!

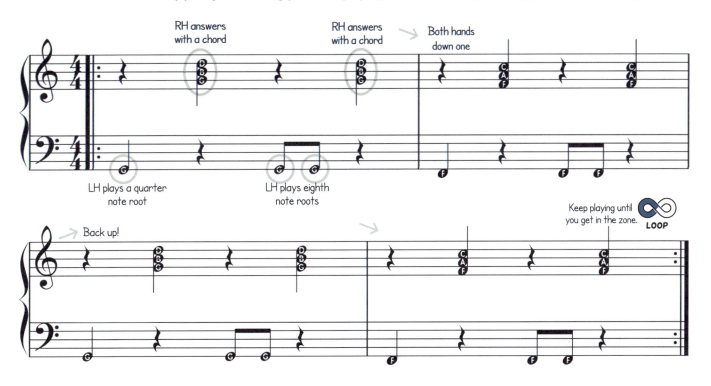

#36. MERRY LANDS

Now play that same progression with a new pattern.

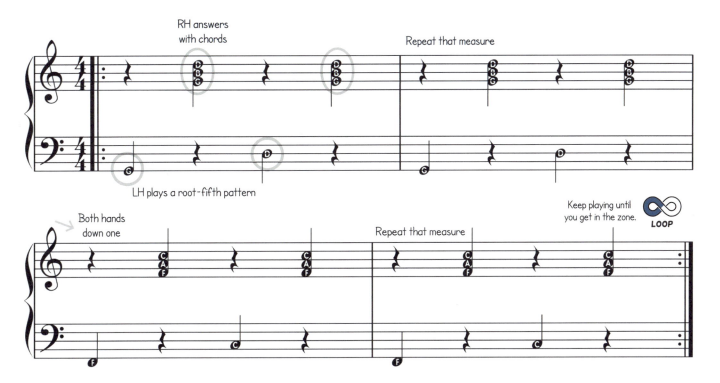

#37. KALEIDOSCOPE SKIES

Take flight and enter a world of magic and enchantment with this song. Your left hand will play a repeating descending bass line while your RH plays a melody, then thirds, then arpeggios. Once you've got it down, compose your own RH part!

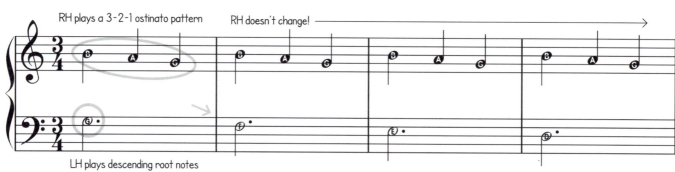

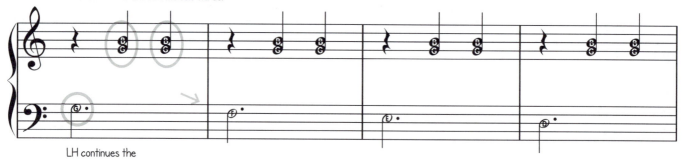

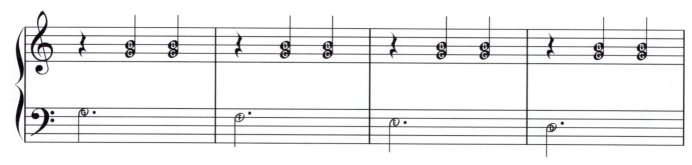

Now play an arpeggio pattern with your right hand...

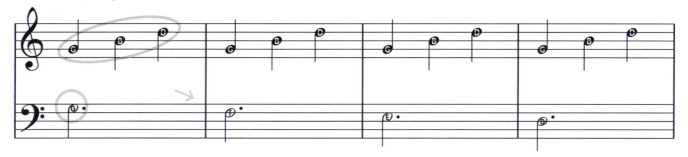

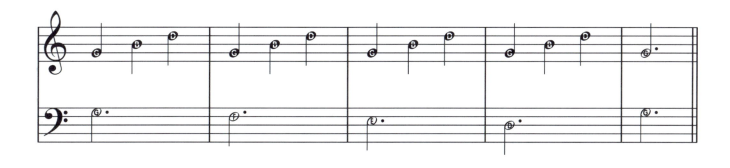

#38. KALEIDOSCOPE VARIATION

Take to the sky! Now create your own melody pattern to play atop the descending left hand pattern. Your right hand will play the same thing each measure. Write in your pattern below!

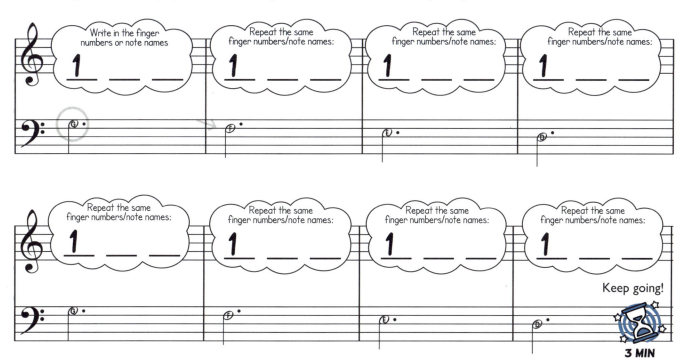

Keep going!

3 MIN

#39. FA LA LA

Imagine this lyrical tune being sung by the inhabitants of a magical mixolydian land. Create a story... or better yet, lyrics! Your right hand will begin the song with a fun melodic sequence followed by a very catchy (be forewarned!) melody, and your left hand will play harmonic fifths. Tip: Try arpeggios in the left hand to sound even more lyrical.

RH plays a 1-3-3, 1-3-3 sequence

Both hands down one! Play the same shape/finger numbers

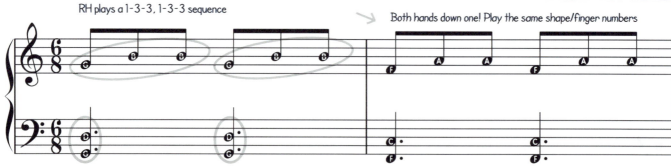

LH plays fifths

Both hands back up!

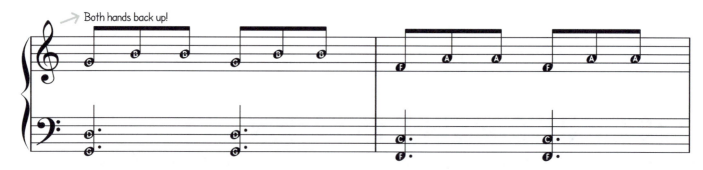

New section! RH plays stepwise melody

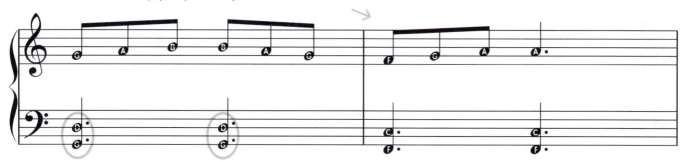

LH continues the fifths pattern from before

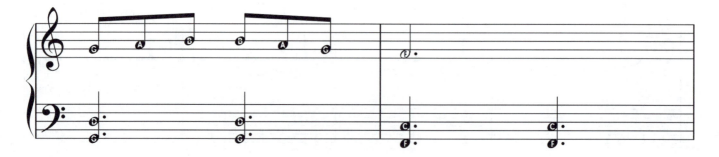

Repeat that section

RH back to the 1-3-3, 1-3-3 sequence   End on dotted half notes

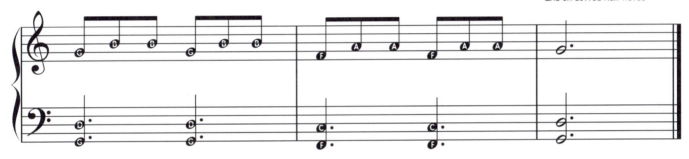

#40. MIXOLYDIAN IMPROV
Now improvise your own melody or pattern over the same LH fifths pattern.

Keep going!

#41. JIG JAMBOREE

Mixolydian is a great mode for jigs! This set of jigs uses droning harmonic fifths for the left hand, and simple but fun-to-play melodic sequences for the right hand.

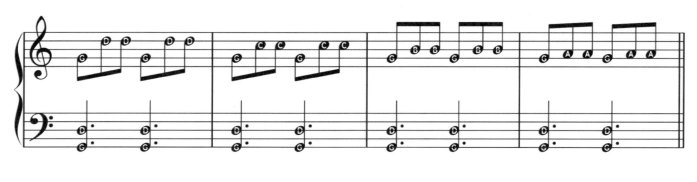

Back to the first pattern!

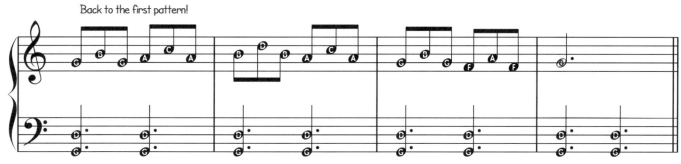

#42. JIG JAM IMPROV

Now improvise your own melody that moves around over the LH droning fifths.

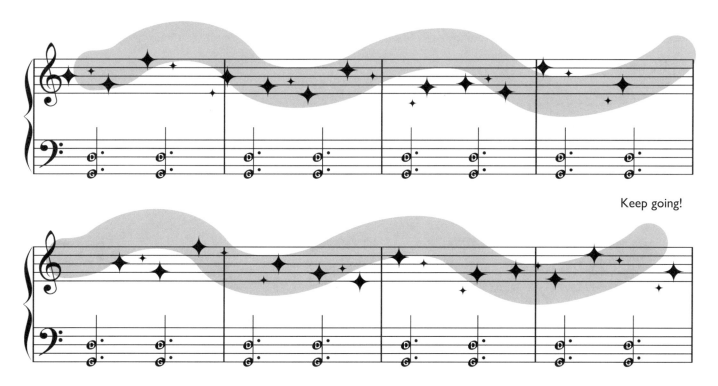

Keep going!

YOU ARE THE PRODUCER!

Music producers are great at prototyping – meaning they make an initial version of something and continue to evolve it into something great. Before moving onto the next mode, prototype an idea inspired by your Mixolydian mode adventures. Then share it with others!

Great music producers try out ideas, get feedback and evolve their project!

#1) CAPTURE

Pick one idea. Now get the rough idea down in some form - a recording, writing notes about it, notating the music or however works for you! Choose a method to capture your idea below.

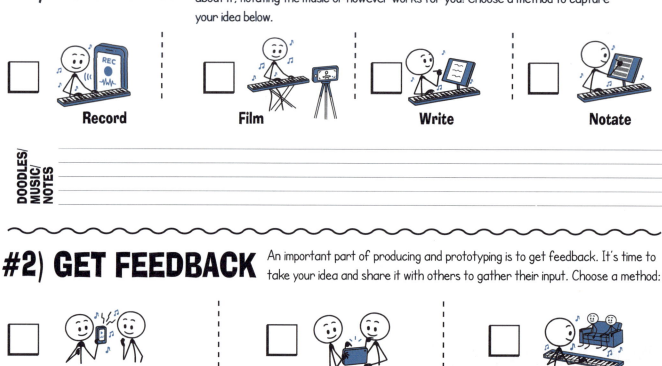

#2) GET FEEDBACK

An important part of producing and prototyping is to get feedback. It's time to take your idea and share it with others to gather their input. Choose a method:

#3) PRESENT!

Take the feedback you received and use it to improve your idea! Once you've got a version you like, share it with others. Choose one of the methods below to share your piece, whether that's making a more polished video or putting on a show! (P.S. - even if it's a short song, a small idea or an imperfect in-process song, sharing is still rewarding and might even inspire others.)

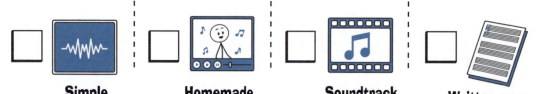

Congratulations! You're ready to move on to Chapter 6!

Psst! Find a printable download of this page at mwfunstuff.com/mode

CHAPTER 6

AEOLIAN MODE

NOW FOR THE DARKNESS AND DEPTH OF AEOLIAN MODE...

A mysterious landscape, a sad sky, a sorcerer's spell... Aeolian mode can convey a wide spectrum of scenes and emotions.

Also known as the natural minor scale, Aeolian mode joins Ionian as the two modes still widely used today. The lowered third of the Aeolian scale adds darkness and depth, while the seventh note of the scale creates a strong mysterious presence.

Welcome to Aeolian mode! This emotive mode has range - it can be scary, sad, mysterious, angry and more!

In this chapter we will focus on feelings like mystery, magic, spookiness and sadness. While the prior chapters focused on soundscape scenes, here we will focus on fantastic characters. Aeolian mode will help create a soundtrack for powerful wizards, nighttime creatures, undersea beings and more.

AEOLIAN MODE: Theory

Aeolian mode can be sad or scary, mad or mysterious!

1. THE SCALE
Here's the Aeolian scale in the key of A (also known as A minor).

On the keyboard:

And on the staff:

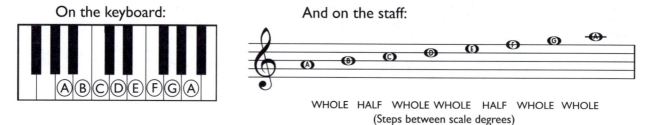

WHOLE   HALF   WHOLE   WHOLE   HALF   WHOLE   WHOLE
(Steps between scale degrees)

2. THE CHORD SCALE
Here's the A Aeolian scale as a chord scale.

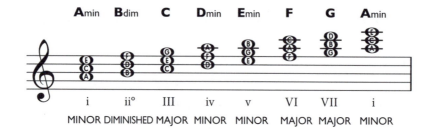

Amin	Bdim	C	Dmin	Emin	F	G	Amin
i	ii°	III	iv	v	VI	VII	i
MINOR	DIMINISHED	MAJOR	MINOR	MINOR	MAJOR	MAJOR	MINOR

3. NOTABLE INTERVALS
Here are the intervals of the scale that give Aeolian Mode its unique sound:

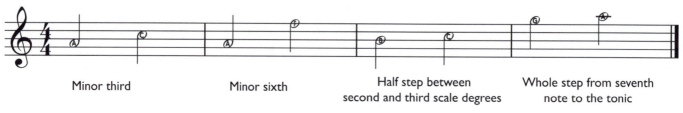

Minor third • Minor sixth • Half step between second and third scale degrees • Whole step from seventh note to the tonic

56 © MERIDEE WINTERS, 2022. ALL RIGHTS RESERVED. MADE WITH CARE BY REAL HUMANS ★ CREATE, DON'T COPY

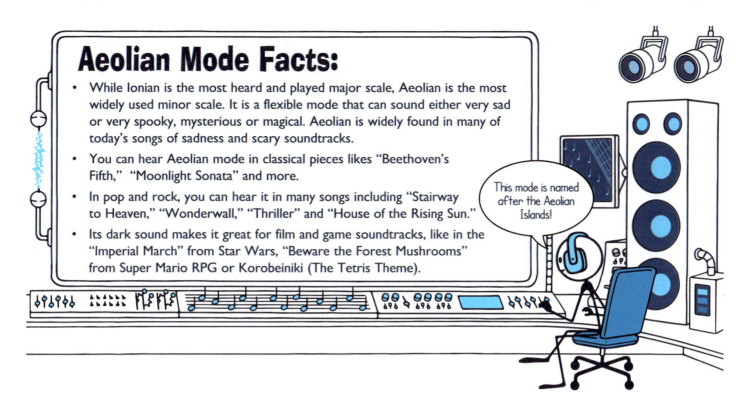

4. HEAR THE DIFFERENCE

Here is "On Top of Old Smokey" in Aeolian mode. How does it sound different than the original? Also try playing "Twinkle, Twinkle Little Star" in Aeolian Mode for a minor twist!

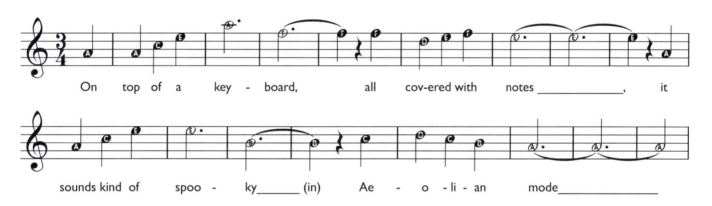

Here are some tips, effects and keyboard sounds to use with Aeolian mode.

- **Aeolian (aka the natural minor scale)** is widely used in dramatic movies, sad movies and also mysterious and even spooky soundtracks.
- **Be dramatic** with keyboard sounds like full strings and orchestral strings or **be mysterious** with lush sounds like those from Lydian mode – sparkly synths and shimmering pads.
- **Be extra spooky** with pipe organ or voice sounds.
- **Be playfully mysterious** with pizzicato strings, harp, accordion, bells or chimes.
- **Avoid "normal" sounds** like horns, woodwinds, guitars and electric piano sounds.
- Try playing the 7th note up a half step - this is also called the harmonic minor scale.

#43. THE SORCERER'S SCALES

Climb to and from the sky with the Aeolian scale. Your right hand will bounce its way from A to A. Then it will reverse that pattern. All the while, your left hand will creep down the Aeolian scale playing octaves.

#44. MYSTERIES OF THE DEEP

"Mysteries of the Deep" and "Mystery Waltz" are variations of "Twinkle, Twinkle Little Star," which is normally in a major key. Can you hear it? We're also using a 3/4 time signature – which is not just used for waltzes, but also for oceanic songs like sea chanties. For this first variation, your left hand will play the melody.

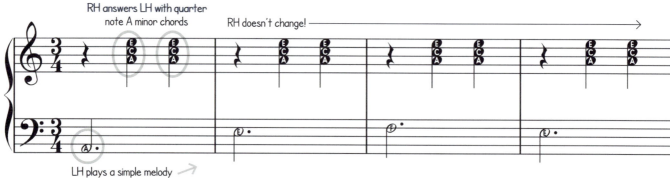

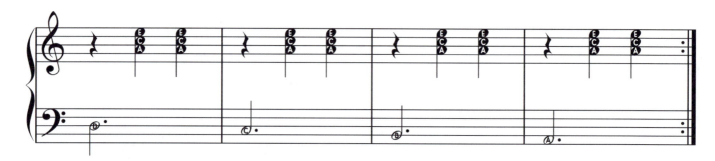

#45. DEEP DIVE IMPROV

Now improvise your own LH dotted-half-note melody. Your RH will continue to echo with A minor chords like above.

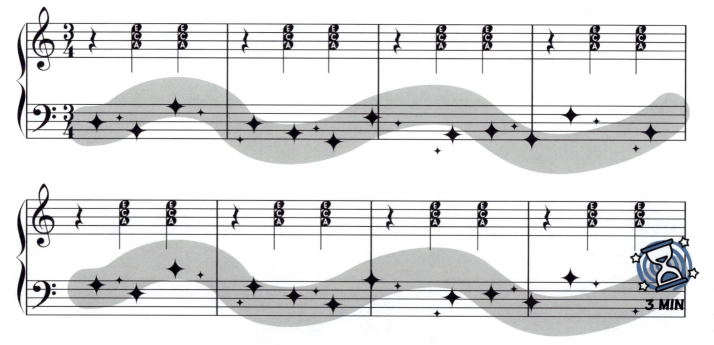

3 MIN

#46. MYSTERY WALTZ

Now your right hand will play the minor "Twinkle, Twinkle Little Star" melody, while your left hand plays a repeating pattern of A minor arpeggios. Try pedal for an extra twinkly effect.

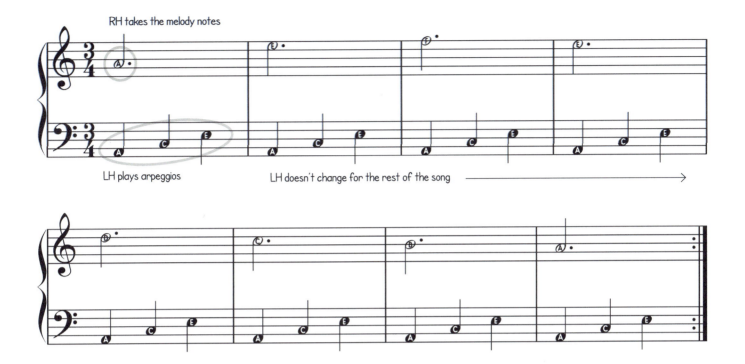

#47. MYSTERY JAM

Now improvise your own melody that moves around over the left hand A minor arpeggios. What story does your minor song tell? What picture does it paint?

MOONLIGHT OSTINATO

For this piece, each section will feature a right hand ostinato part. (That means a part that repeats with the same notes and patterns while the left hand changes.) The repetition adds to the eerie, ominous feeling of Aeolian mode.

#48. VARIATION #1: RH plays an arpeggio pattern

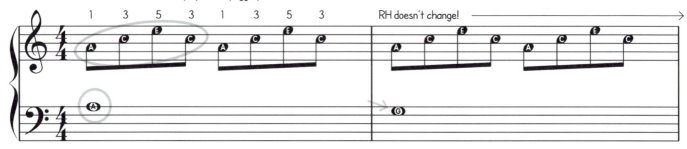

LH plays a descending line of root notes.

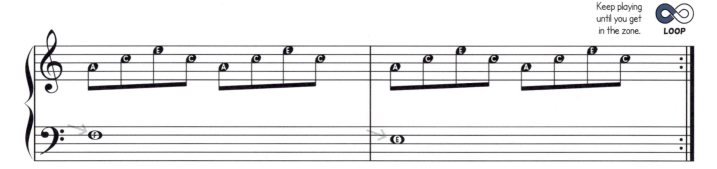

Keep playing until you get in the zone. LOOP

#49. VARIATION #2: RH plays an ostinato pattern

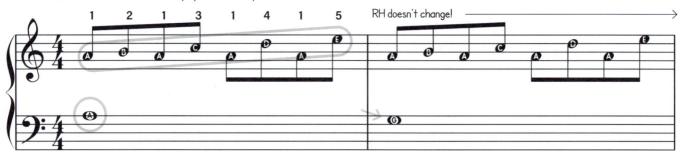

LH back up! Repeat the descending bass line.

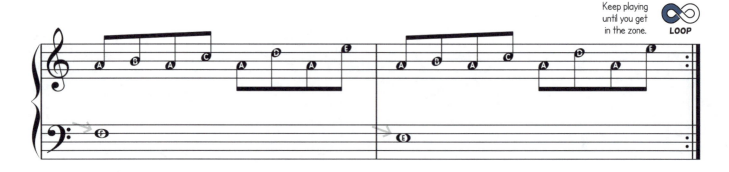

Keep playing until you get in the zone. LOOP

#50. VARIATION #3: RH plays a different ostinato pattern   RH doesn't change!

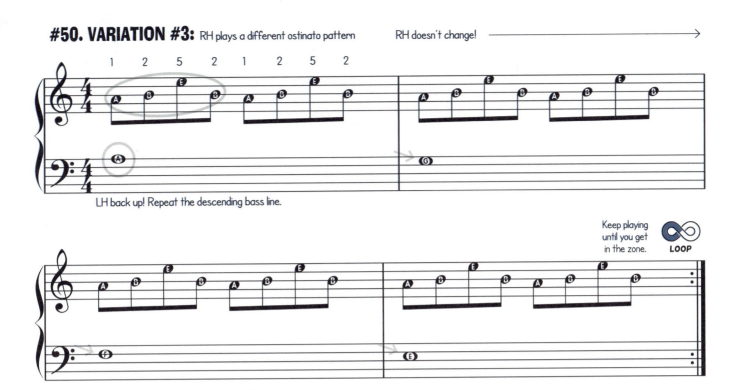

LH back up! Repeat the descending bass line.

Keep playing until you get in the zone. LOOP

#51. MOONLIGHT OSTINATO: YOUR VARIATION

Make your own Aeolian composition! Create your own ostinato pattern by writing in finger numbers below. Your left hand will continue playing the descending bass line.

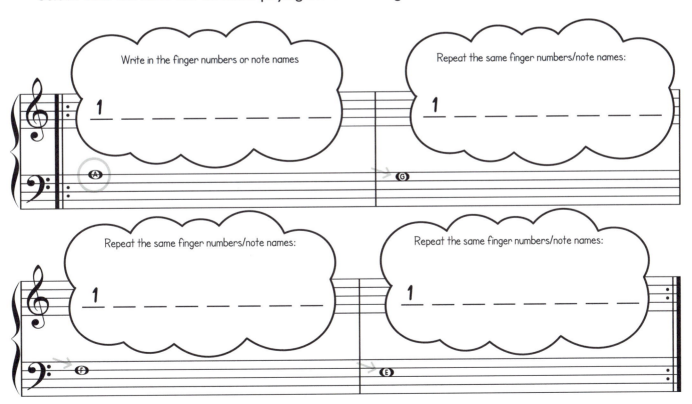

#52. NIGHT FLIGHT

Thirds and fifths are simple but powerful intervals, and this song combines them for suspenseful results. Your left hand will play an ostinato pattern of melodic fifths, while your right hand wanders up and down in melodic thirds.

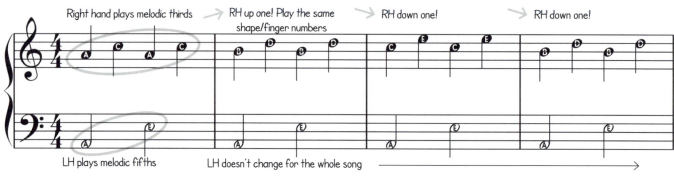

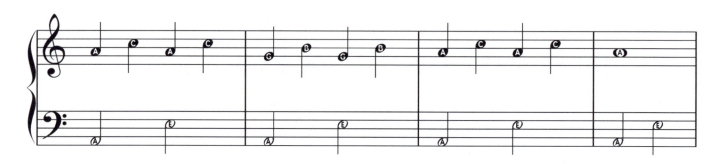

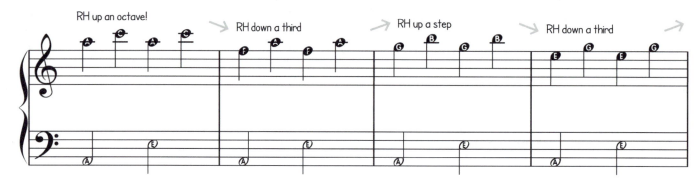

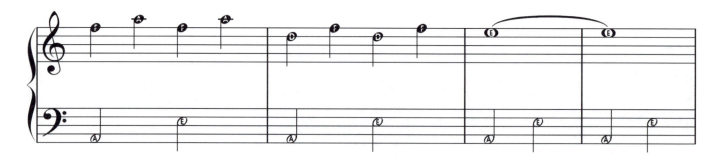

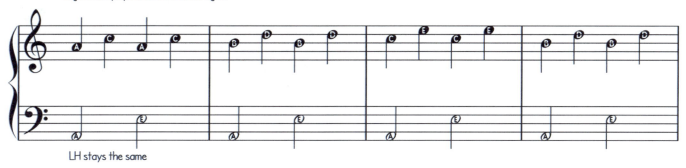

Right hand plays the first section again

LH stays the same

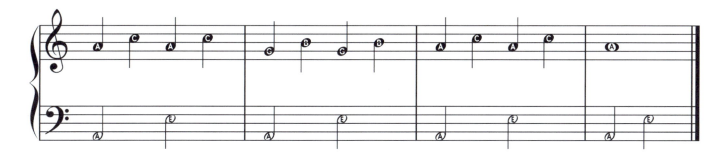

#53. NIGHT FLIGHT IMPROV

Improvise! Explore the keys with the right hand thirds while your left hand continues the pattern. Then break free and play whatever you feel!

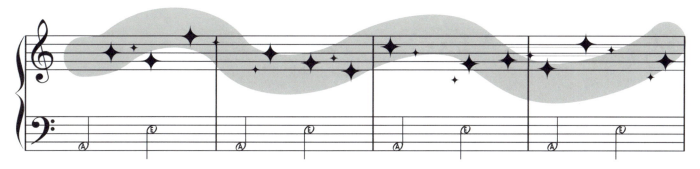

Keep going!

3 MIN

#54. ELF LEGEND

Aeolian mode is not just for magic and mystery– it can also convey great sadness. In this somber soundtrack song, your left hand will play a roof-fifth-octave pattern while your right hand plays chords. Both hands will move together through the melancholy chord progression. Then, the right hand will shift to a simple but moving melody.

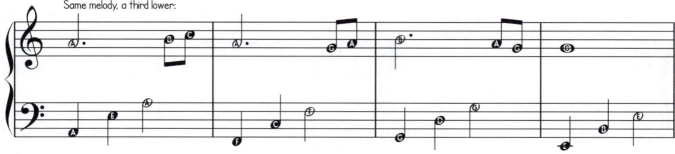

#55. COMPOSE YOUR OWN SONG: _____

Psst! Find a printable download of this page at mwfunstuff.com/mode

Now write in your own melody to that same rhythm to play over the same LH chord pattern. (Write in letters or finger numbers). See our example on the right.

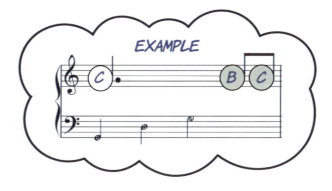

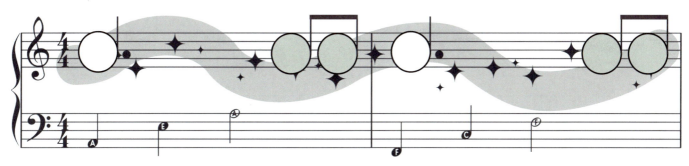

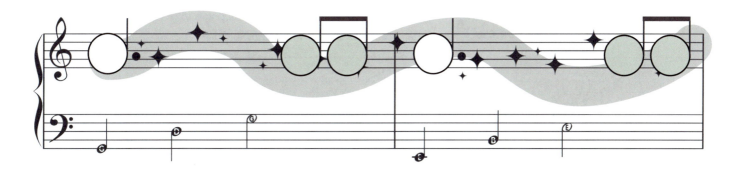

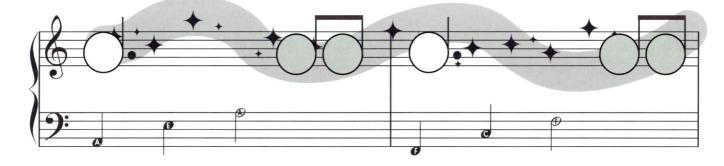

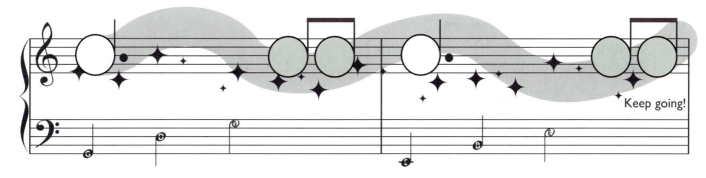

Keep going!

YOU ARE THE PRODUCER!

Music producers are great at prototyping — meaning they make an initial version of something and continue to evolve it into something great. Before moving onto the next mode, prototype an idea inspired by your Aeolian mode adventures. Then share it with others!

Great music producers try out ideas, get feedback and evolve their project!

#1) CAPTURE

Pick one idea. Now get the rough idea down in some form - a recording, writing notes about it, notating the music or however works for you! Choose a method to capture your idea below.

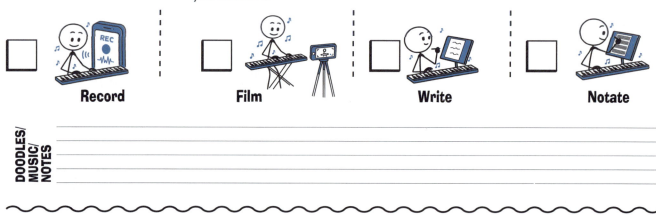

☐ Record   ☐ Film   ☐ Write   ☐ Notate

DOODLES/ MUSIC/ NOTES
_____
_____
_____
_____

#2) GET FEEDBACK

An important part of producing and prototyping is to get feedback. It's time to take your idea and share it with others to gather their input. Choose a method:

☐ Play a recording   ☐ Play a video   ☐ Perform for Others

FEEDBACK/ NOTES

#3) PRESENT!

Take the feedback you received and use it to improve your idea! Once you've got a version you like, share it with others. Choose one of the methods below to share your piece, whether that's making a more polished video or putting on a show! (P.S. - even if it's a short song, a small idea or an imperfect in-process song, sharing is still rewarding and might even inspire others.)

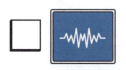    

☐ Simple Recording   ☐ Homemade Movie   ☐ Soundtrack   ☐ Written song   ☐ Show

Congratulations! You're ready to move on to Chapter 7!

Psst! Find a printable download of this page at mwfunstuff.com/mode

CHAPTER 7
LOCRIAN MODE

NOW FOR VEXING, PERPLEXING LOCRIAN MODE!

Only one chapter left until our grand finale chapter. But first, a quick stop in Locrian Mode.

Why so quick? Locrian Mode is rarely used and is considered to be unsettling, confusing and perplexing. Some people describe Locrian mode as sounding tense, unfinished, creepy, dark and puzzling.

While it is rarely used and wouldn't make a strong main theme, it may just be a good fit for a soundtrack scene that is unnerving or unusual. (From scary villains to far out alien worlds, creatures and more!) For your last mode – and soundtrack – you will head to a place that feels unsettling or confusing. Then it's on to the final chapter! (Hint: curious what that final chapter will be? Well, just like comic book fans go to a comic book convention, our final chapter is a creativity convention… called Create-o-con!)

Welcome to Locrian Mode, little used and VERY different!

1. THE SCALE
Here's the Locrian scale in the key of B.

On the keyboard:

And on the staff:

B C D E F G A B

HALF WHOLE WHOLE HALF WHOLE WHOLE WHOLE
(Steps between scale degrees)

2. THE CHORD SCALE
Here's the B Locrian scale as a chord scale.

i°	II	iii	iv	V	VI	vii	i°
DIMINISHED	MAJOR	MINOR	MINOR	MAJOR	MAJOR	MINOR	DIMINISHED

3. NOTABLE INTERVALS
Here are the interval of the scale that give Locrian mode its unique sound:

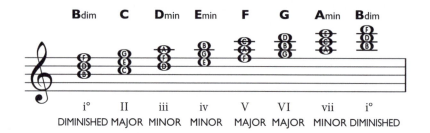

Minor second   Diminished (lowered) fifth   Half step between fourth and fifth

Locrian Mode Facts:

- One interval that makes Locrian unsettling is the diminished fifth - which is enharmonically the same (sounds the same) as an augmented fourth – also known as the tritone. Because of its unstable sound, the tritone was forbidden in classical music for a period of time.
- You can hear Locrian mode used in "Guitar Hero" by Rush and "Army of Me" by Bjork.

4. HEAR THE DIFFERENCE

Here is "On Top of Old Smokey" in Locrian mode. How does it sound different than the original?

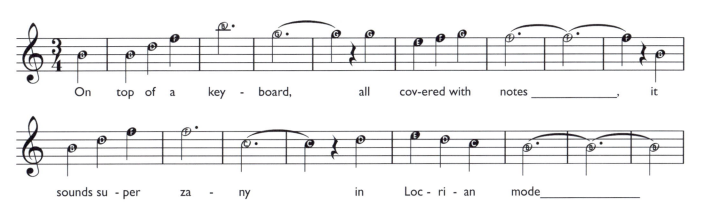

On top of a key - board, all cov-ered with notes _____, it sounds su - per za - ny in Loc - ri - an mode_____

Locrian mode is rarely used in songs. Go ahead and experiment however you want.

Because Locrian Mode is rarely used, use this space to write or draw strange scenes or character ideas, to take notes or to jot down sounds you want to try.

#56. PERPLEXING PLANET

Explore this strange-sounding planet by going up and down the B Locrian scale. Your left hand will play an ostinato pattern of B diminished arpeggios, while your RH creeps up, then down the scale in dotted half notes.

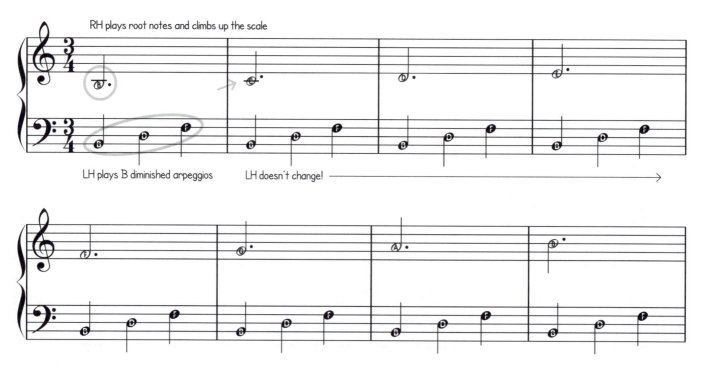

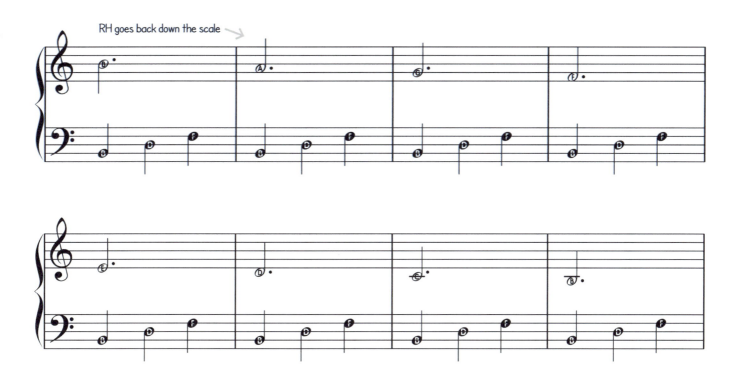

#57. INTERPLANETARY IMPROV

Now it's time to improvise in this perplexing mode! Improvise with your right hand while your left hand continues the pattern of B diminished arpeggios.

YOU ARE THE PRODUCER!

Music producers are great at prototyping – meaning they make an initial version of something and continue to evolve it into something great. Before moving onto the next mode, prototype an idea inspired by your Locrian mode adventures. Then share it with others!

Great music producers try out ideas, get feedback and evolve their project!

#1) CAPTURE

Pick one idea. Now get the rough idea down in some form - a recording, writing notes about it, notating the music or however works for you! Choose a method to capture your idea below.

☐ Record   ☐ Film   ☐ Write   ☐ Notate

DOODLES/MUSIC/NOTES
_____
_____
_____
_____

#2) GET FEEDBACK

An important part of producing and prototyping is to get feedback. It's time to take your idea and share it with others to gather their input. Choose a method:

☐ Play a recording   ☐ Play a video   ☐ Perform for Others

FEEDBACK/NOTES
_____
_____

#3) PRESENT!

Take the feedback you received and use it to improve your idea! Once you've got a version you like, share it with others. Choose one of the methods below to share your piece, whether that's making a more polished video or putting on a show! (P.S. - even if it's a short song, a small idea or an imperfect in-process song, sharing is still rewarding and might even inspire others.)

☐ Simple Recording   ☐ Homemade Movie   ☐ Soundtrack   ☐ Written song   ☐ Show

Congrats! You're ready to move on to the FINAL CHAPTER!

Psst! Find a printable download of this page at mwfunstuff.com/mode

© MERIDEE WINTERS, 2022. ALL RIGHTS RESERVED.   MADE WITH CARE BY REAL HUMANS ★ CREATE, DON'T COPY

CHAPTER 8

CREATE-O-CON

Welcome to the final chapter of your mode adventure — and to the creative event of the season. You have learned about all seven modes, created your own soundtracks and earned yourself a ticket to Create-o-con.

At this convention, creators of all types gather to attend events, get inspired, create and even compete! In this chapter you'll participate in three events that use your mode knowledge and creative skills to create new, exciting projects.

Get ready to make music, videos and more... at Create-o-con!

P.S. – Don't forget to check out mwfunstuff.com/mode for downloadable activities from this chapter!

"Welcome to the creative event of the season!"

Tips: Try narrating as you play. For characters, think of actions. What are they doing next? Where are they going? Be free and create!

SONG-A-THON

EVENT #2

For this next event, you'll create your own original song by combining sections. In music, the structure/order of these sections is what we call the "song form."

Sections are traditionally labeled "A," "B," "C" and so on, and typical song forms include A-B-C-A, A-B-B-A, A-B-A-B-C-B and more. For this activity, you'll create the sections and choose the order (song form). Don't worry! We'll walk you through it.

First: Choose your mode/chord progression

If you need a refresher on how to play these chords, review the chord scales in each mode's theory studio!

Psst! Find a printable download of this page at mwfunstuff.com/mode

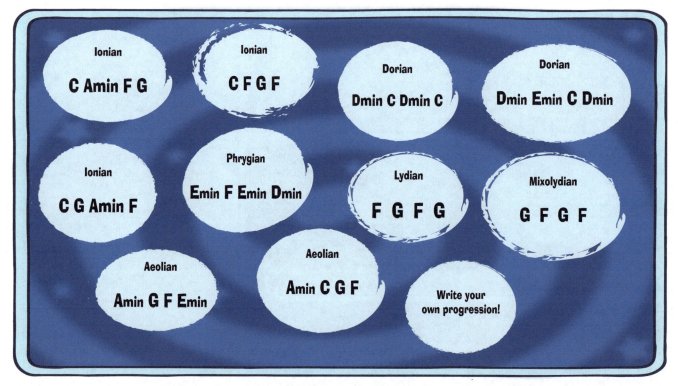

Ionian — C Amin F G
Ionian — C F G F
Dorian — Dmin C Dmin C
Dorian — Dmin Emin C Dmin
Ionian — C G Amin F
Phrygian — Emin F Emin Dmin
Lydian — F G F G
Mixolydian — G F G F
Aeolian — Amin G F Emin
Aeolian — Amin C G F
Write your own progression!

Your progression: (Write it in here.) ☐ ☐ ☐ ☐

Now copy it into the square boxes in the A and B sections on the next page.

Next: Warm up by practicing improvising over your chord progression

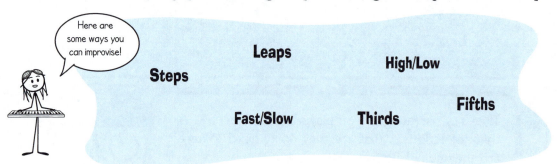

Here are some ways you can improvise!

Steps   Leaps   High/Low
Fast/Slow   Thirds   Fifths

You're ready to create your song on the next page!

#59. MY SONG: _____

A SECTION: LH CHORDS, THEN RH CHORDS

Write the chords from your progression into the square chord symbol boxes. Play chords with your LH, then right hand. Move to the next hand/chord position in your progression and play chords again.

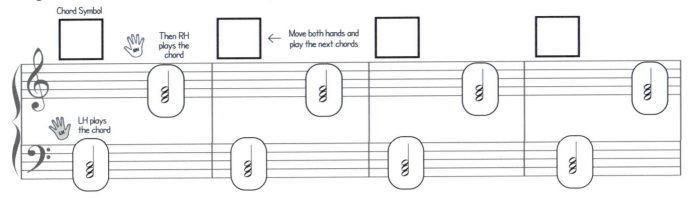

B SECTION: LEFT HAND FIFTH + RIGHT HAND PATTERN

Write your own finger number pattern in the first cloud below. Then copy it into the other clouds. Move both hands with each chord change and play a left hand fifth + your RH pattern in that position.

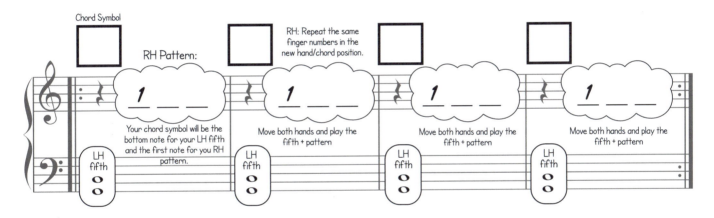

C SECTION: LEFT HAND FIFTH + RIGHT HAND IMPROV

Your LH can just repeat the tonic chord (the first chord from your progression) OR play the same thing it did in the B section: harmonic fifths, moving through the chord progression. Your RH will improvise!

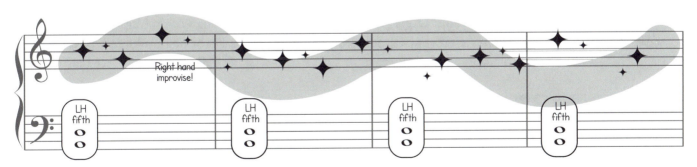

ARRANGE IT: Choose the song form/order for playing your sections.

☐ ABCA   ☐ ABABCB   ☐ ABBA   ☐ Other: _____

EVENT #3 — PRODUCER-PALOOZA

#60. PRODUCER-PALOOZA

The final event of Create-o-con is a conference favorite: a competition where creators enter their own soundtracks (music+video) and premiere them for an enthusiastic crowd!

To compete, you'll record and share your own song along with a video. Choose from the options below... and see if you'll take the top prize!

SONG: Which song will you choose?

☐ Your ABCA song from the previous page

☐ A different song you've written: _____

VISUALS: What visuals will show on your video?

☐ **Bronze Medal:** A single favorite image (from this book or beyond) that shows for the whole video/song.

☐ **Silver Medal:** Create a gallery of photos to set to music. Extra points for adding effects and transitions.

☐ **Gold Medal:** Create your own visuals for the video, such as your own artwork, video footage of your friends/yourself, nature and more. Go wild.

PRODUCTION: How will you assemble your project?

☐ **Ruby Level:** Record yourself on a voice memo app or other app and import it into a movie app to add images. Share with others electronically.

☐ **Emerald Level:** Record yourself with backing musicians.

☐ **Extra Credit:** Use a recording app to create a song with multiple tracks/layers. Experiment with backing tracks, recording multiple tracks of yourself, and more.

BROADCAST AND SHARE: Present your film to others.

Who did you share it with? _____
When did you share it? _____
How did you share it? (Email? Movie night?) _____

Psst! Send your video to Meridee and get a prize in the mail! Books@merideewinters.com

FILM SCREENING TODAY

Find a printable version of this page at mwfunstuff.com/mode

© MERIDEE WINTERS, 2022. ALL RIGHTS RESERVED.   MADE WITH CARE BY REAL HUMANS ★ CREATE, DON'T COPY

CREATE-O-CON
Take it further

Keep going! Use your creative skills to make even more videos, music and projects.

Congratulations! You completed all three events and accomplished so much at Create-o-con. You're done this book... but keep on creating! Here are some real-world ways to take the creative magic with you to inspire others.

Make a video gift for someone: Use your new video and production skills to send someone a musical, video surprise.

Learn Recording Software: Expand your skills with recording music, adding tracks and more.

Jam with others: Try improvising, playing or writing music with others.

Make a soundtrack for an event: Create music for a haunted house, holiday gathering and more!

Pet sounds: Make a soundtrack video with pictures of a beloved pet!

Your idea: What other creative musical projects could you take on?

Made in United States
Troutdale, OR
05/08/2024